New Directions for
Higher Education

Betsy O. Barefoot
Jillian L. Kinzie
CO-EDITORS

Increasing Diversity in Doctoral Education: Implications for Theory and Practice

Karri A. Holley
Joretta Joseph
EDITORS

Number 163 • Fall 2013
Jossey-Bass
San Francisco

INCREASING DIVERSITY IN DOCTORAL EDUCATION: IMPLICATIONS FOR THEORY
AND PRACTICE
Karri A. Holley, Joretta Joseph
New Directions for Higher Education, no. 163
Betsy O. Barefoot and Jillian L. Kinzie, Co-editors

Microfilm copies of issues and articles are available in 16mm and 35mm,
as well as microfiche in 105mm, through University Microfilms Inc., 300
North Zeeb Road, Ann Arbor, MI 48106-1346.

NEW DIRECTIONS FOR HIGHER EDUCATION (ISSN 0271-0560, electronic
ISSN 1536-0741) is part of The Jossey-Bass Higher and Adult Education
Series and is published quarterly by Wiley Subscription Services, Inc.,
A Wiley Company, at Jossey-Bass, One Montgomery Street, Suite 1200,
San Francisco, CA 94104-4594. POSTMASTER: Send address changes to
New Directions for Higher Education, Jossey-Bass, One Montgomery
Street, Suite 1200, San Francisco, CA 94104-4594.

New Directions for Higher Education is indexed in Current Index to Journals in Education (ERIC); Higher Education Abstracts.

Individual subscription rate (in USD): $89 per year US/Can/Mex, $113
rest of world; institutional subscription rate: $311 US, $351 Can/Mex,
$385 rest of world. Single copy rate: $29. Electronic only–all regions:
$89 individual, $311 institutional; Print & Electronic–US: $98 individ-
ual, $357 institutional; Print & Electronic–Canada/Mexico: $98
individual, $397 institutional; Print & Electronic–Rest of World:
$122 individual, $431 institutional.

Editorial correspondence should be sent to the Co-editor,
Betsy O. Barefoot, Gardner Institute, Box 72, Brevard, NC 28712.

Cover photograph © Digital Vision

www.josseybass.com

CONTENTS

Editors' Notes

The significance of a diverse doctoral student enrollment cannot be underestimated. By supporting diversity across the academic disciplines, universities ensure that the nation's intellectual capacities and opportunities are fully realized (Council of Graduate Schools, 2007; National Science Foundation, 2011). Since doctoral-degree recipients go on to assume roles as faculty and other educators, the implications for the academic workforce are also significant. Yet universities are increasingly hampered in their efforts to recruit, retain, and graduate a diverse doctoral student population. The reduction in institutional, state, and federal financial support; the troubled academic pipeline from undergraduate to graduate studies for certain student populations; and the emergence of new legal obstacles related to student recruitment have hindered efforts to increase doctoral student diversity (Garces, 2012).

In this volume, we consider diversity broadly across doctoral education. Diversity is defined as those numerous elements of difference between groups of people that play significant roles in social institutions, including race and ethnicity, gender, socioeconomic class, sexual orientation, and culture, among others (Smith, 2009). Chapter authors address how issues of diversity intersect with and have an impact on doctoral students across multiple disciplines. The chapters seek to offer new insights as to the significance of diversity for doctoral education. In doing so, our intent is to demonstrate how diversity operates through multiple venues and definitions. The goal of the volume is twofold: one, to provide a conceptual framework for understanding the influence of diversity on the doctoral student experience as well as the challenges of fostering diversity within the institutional milieu; and two, to offer recommendations for practice based on scholarship and firsthand experience from researchers in the field.

The scholars who serve as authors for this volume represent leading researchers from multiple disciplines. A number of them presented sessions at the Mini-Symposium on Women of Color in STEM (Science, Technology, Engineering, and Math), sponsored by the National Science Foundation in 2009. Their conversations provided the impetus for this volume.

Scope and Purpose

The doctoral degree has gained increased attention from higher education administrators, policy groups, and researchers over the last three decades (Bowen & Rudenstine, 1992; Golde, 2005; Lovitts, 2001; Walker, Golde, Jones, Bueschel, & Hutchings, 2008; Woodrow Wilson Foundation, 2005). This interest emphasizes the crucial role that the doctorate plays in the higher education system. Doctoral programs train future faculty, administrators, and other national leaders, who construct a variety of academic, research, and professional careers. The doctorate holds a key role in the country's scientific ambition, future economic security, and knowledge production (Gardner & Mendoza, 2010). Given its significance, doctoral education is an essential area for analysis and discussion. As summarized in a 2007 report by the Council of Graduate Schools, such efforts ensure that "knowledge creators and innovators of tomorrow have the cultural awareness, skills, and expertise to compete effectively in a knowledge-based global economy" (p. 1).

Researchers have focused on numerous facets of the doctoral student experience, including time to degree, financial support, the impact of the undergraduate institution, and postgraduation outcomes. In particular, concern has been expressed over the lack of student diversity in doctoral programs (Council of Graduate Schools, 2004; National Science Foundation, 2008). The National Science Foundation (2008) recently issued a report on diversity in graduate education, concluding that "the creative engagement of diverse ideas and perspectives is essential to enabling the transformative research that invigorates our nation's scientific and engineering enterprise" (p. 1). A wealth of data has supported the influential impact of diversity on student development in higher education, although such data largely reflects the undergraduate student experience. Yet doctoral students also engage in a developmental process as part of their degree program. The engagement of diverse individuals and perspectives offers tremendous potential for knowledge advancement. Diversity throughout the curriculum and the professoriate also represents the ability of higher education to reflect the complexity of American society for future generations of students.

Diversity, of course, is a topic that influences all aspects of higher education. Most commonly, scholarship in this area examines single-race or gendered experiences and their relationship to diversity or focuses specifically on the undergraduate student. One underlying principle regarding diversity research is that individuals interact with the institution in different ways depending on their unique characteristics. Simply increasing enrollment numbers related to a diverse student population does not ensure that students will benefit from interactions with diverse others. Rather, faculty and administrators should be cognizant of both informal and classroom diversity (Gurin, Dey, Hurtado, & Gurin, 2002). For doctoral education, these characteristics suggest that the ability "to perceive differences both within groups and between groups" is essential to critical thinking, knowledge generation, and knowledge advancement (Gurin et al., 2002, p. 360).

This volume fills an important niche in terms of the conversation related to doctoral education and student diversity. The topic is a significant one, as evidenced by policy decisions, media coverage, and institutional behavior. We approached the topic with the assumptions that diversity is comprised of multiple and intersecting variables and that these variables play out in unique ways across the academic disciplines. When reviewing the extant literature on doctoral education and diversity, we suggest that higher education researchers should broaden the scope of their focus. Just as socialization happens in unique forms across different disciplines, so do definitions of and engagement with diversity vary across the same disciplines. In addition, doctoral students enter their graduate education shaped by a wealth of previous educational involvement. They also interact with professional associations, policymakers, institutional administrators, and community members. Each of these groups contributes to the unique student experience, and each defines (or should define) in some way our definition of diversity.

Chapter Outline

Lisa M. Frehill and Rachel Ivie begin the volume by expanding our concept of doctoral education. They examine how professional societies collect and disseminate data specific to diversity in terms of doctoral students and faculty. This often untapped empirical resource provides a rich context to understanding not only the role that diversity plays in terms of graduate education, but also how diversity continues to have an impact on professors in their scholarly career. It is from these data-driven efforts that scholars interested in doctoral education might see how diversity plays out in specific disciplines and across various career stages. Such understanding only underscores the importance of diversity across doctoral programs.

Collaborating between and among higher education institutions, professional associations, and policy groups is further examined in Chapter 2. Kelly Mack, Claudia Rankins, and Kamilah Woodson outline the trajectory of minority scholars through the academic pipeline towards the doctorate. They specifically consider the challenge of achieving parity in terms of proportional student enrollment that is representative of the larger U.S. demographic. The authors introduce a career identity development model that considers the intersection of multiple identities as well as how underrepresented minority doctoral students and faculty members might support each other across institutional and organizational boundaries.

Elsa C. Ruiz considers the academic pipeline for Latina students in STEM disciplines in Chapter 3. Given the national conversation regarding increasing the number of STEM graduates and diversifying recipients of STEM doctorates, Ruiz's work reminds us that educational challenges begin well before enrollment in a doctoral program. She specifically considers how early engagement with mathematics, a field that is considered a key to a future successful academic career, can influence the achievement of underrepresented student populations. Latina doctoral students face unique challenges related to familial roles and expectations as well as community norms regarding gender and achievement. One implication of Ruiz's chapter is that the examination of doctoral education should consider more than the timeframe of actual graduate school enrollment and also be aware how student experiences with key academic disciplines shape an emergent academic identity.

Susan K. Gardner focuses on the experiences of first-generation doctoral students in Chapter 4. By emphasizing the perspectives of an often-unrecognized and "invisible" minority student population, Gardner argues that diversity operates beyond single or visible categories of difference. First-generation doctoral students are shaped by their previous academic preparation, family expectations, financial resources, and career aspirations in ways that are different from their non-first-generation peers. Higher education institutions must actively define and engage with this population to enrich the diversity of their graduate student enrollment.

In Chapter 5, Jaime Lester considers the challenges faced by many doctoral students in terms of work–life balance. The scarcity of family-friendly policies for this population, including paid medical or family leave, can present obstacles for both male and female students. In particular, Lester suggests that the progressive policies developed for tenure-track or tenured faculty over the last decade have neglected doctoral students. Such students are often caught in an uncertain role between that of an undergraduate student and a full-time "employee," meaning that work as a graduate teaching or research assistant offers little security. Beyond the issue of formal policies, doctoral students can experience challenges in finding faculty role models who offer examples of a successful work–life balance appropriate to the discipline and the institution.

Unique institutional types are explored by Joretta Joseph in Chapter 6. Joseph considers the important role that historically Black colleges and universities (HBCUs) play in advancing the academic careers of minority scholars, specifically those within STEM disciplines. HBCUs serve a prominent role in educating minority women who later complete a doctoral degree. Joseph offers examples of distinctive institutional characteristics that students experience at a historically Black institution and considers how other institutional types might provide similar benefits for underrepresented students. Beyond institutional type, Joseph's chapter underscores the notion that students begin their journey towards the doctorate before graduate school enrollment. Researchers should consider how those formative experiences shape diversity in doctoral programs.

Eva Graham further considers institutional type in Chapter 7 by considering minority doctoral students at elite private research universities. Drawing on her professional background working at such an institution, Graham illustrates challenges that minority doctoral students might encounter related to admission, coursework, research opportunities, and faculty mentors. She also suggests that faculty at such institutions bear a significant responsibility for engaging underrepresented students in their research laboratories and grant-funded endeavors, which are essential to a future faculty career.

In Chapter 8, Ketevan Mamiseishvili introduces an unacknowledged aspect of diversity in doctoral education: the interaction between doctoral students and foreign-born faculty. Such faculty members often introduce issues such as internationalization and globalization into the curriculum. Mamiseishvili uses existing data to document the high research productivity of this faculty population and considers what advantages doctoral students might gain from scholarly interaction. She also notes that such faculty tend to work in international collaborations more than their U.S. peers, which suggests increased avenues of networking and scholarship for doctoral students.

Karri A. Holley offers the final chapter, which brings together questions of diversity related to knowledge production and identity development, both crucial aspects of doctoral education. She considers how diversity in multiple forms offers advantages toward innovation, creativity, and critical awareness. Holley outlines implications for faculty and administrators interested in the practice of doctoral education and concludes with questions for future research and policy in this area.

Conclusion

We anticipate that this volume will appeal to three overlapping audiences: first, those scholars who focus on doctoral education; second, individuals interested in diversity in higher education; and third, faculty and administrators seeking to better understand diversity in their doctoral programs. Certainly doctoral education as an area of study in higher education has grown exponentially over the last few decades. Efforts of policy groups and government agencies to better understand the doctoral student experience (including the Carnegie Initiative on the Doctorate, the Woodrow Wilson Foundation's Responsive PhD Project, and projects from the National Science Foundation) have been numerous; other initiatives include the development of a Special Interest Group with the American Educational Research Association focused on doctoral education, as well as several new journals devoted to the topic. The audience for issues related to diversity in higher education is also broad, and encompasses numerous scholarly communities. The question of diversity has been prevalent in numerous recent legal decisions. A 2011 document released by the U.S. Department of Education offered explicit ways in which higher education can foster diversity, concluding that "attaining a diverse student body is at the heart of a university's proper institutional mission" (p. 1). How colleges and universities can foster a diverse student population is inevitably related to the benefits of diversity, which make this volume important.

This volume represents an effort to compile chapters that reflect multiple perspectives on diversity, not only in terms of race and ethnicity, but also institutional type, academic discipline, and national origin. No single direction towards increasing diversity is correct. Rather, by expanding our notion of diversity and understanding the multiple venues through which it occurs, we hope to stimulate conversation about a key aspect of American higher education.

Karri A. Holley
Joretta Joseph
Editors

References

Bowen, W., & Rudenstine, N. (1992). *In pursuit of the PhD.* Princeton, NJ: Princeton University Press.

Council of Graduate Schools. (2004). *PhD completion and attrition: Policy numbers, leadership, and next steps.* Washington, DC: Author.

Council of Graduate Schools. (2007). *Broadening participation in graduate education.* Washington, DC: Author.

Garces, L. (2012). Racial diversity, legitimacy, and the citizenry: The impact of affirmative action bans on graduate school enrollment. *Review of Higher Education, 36*(1), 93–132.

Gardner, S., & Mendoza, P. (Eds.). (2010). *On becoming a scholar: Socialization and development in doctoral education.* Sterling, VA: Stylus Publishing.

Golde, C. (2005). The role of the department and discipline in doctoral student attrition: Lessons from four departments. *Journal of Higher Education, 76*(6), 669–700.

Gurin, P., Dey, E., Hurtado, S., & Gurin, G. (2002). Diversity in higher education: Theory and impact on educational outcomes. *Harvard Educational Review, 72*(3), 330–366.

Lovitts, B. (2001). *Leaving the ivory tower.* Lanham, MD: Rowman & Littlefield.

National Science Foundation. (2008). *Broadening participation at the National Science Foundation: A framework for action.* Washington, DC: Author.

National Science Foundation. (2011). *Measuring diversity: An evaluation guide for STEM graduate program leaders.* Washington, DC: Author.

Smith, D. (2009). *Diversity's promise for higher education: Making it work.* Baltimore, MD: Johns Hopkins University Press.

U.S. Department of Education. (2011). Guidance on the voluntary use of race to achieve diversity in postsecondary education. Retrieved from www.justice.gov/crt/about/edu/documents/guidancepost.pdf

Walker, G., Golde, C., Jones, L., Bueschel, A., & Hutchings, P. (2008). *The formation of scholars: Doctoral education in the 21st century.* San Francisco, CA: Jossey-Bass.

Woodrow Wilson Foundation. (2005). *The responsive PhD: Innovations in doctoral education.* Princeton, NJ: Author.

KARRI A. HOLLEY *is associate professor and coordinator of the Higher Education Program at the University of Alabama, where she also serves on the advisory board for the Tide Together Graduate Student Mentoring Program.*

JORETTA JOSEPH *is the program administrator and graduate advisor for the National Physical Science Consortium.*

1

Professional societies collect a wealth of data on underrepresented scholars in specific disciplines that can be used to understand minority experiences throughout different stages of academia.

Increasing the Visibility of Women of Color in Academic Science and Engineering: Professional Society Data

Lisa M. Frehill, Rachel Ivie

There has been much recent interest in improving the U.S. infrastructure for science, technology, engineering, and mathematics (STEM) in general and in addressing persistent gaps in representation based on gender and race/ethnicity in STEM fields. Several important reports by the National Academies have called attention to the issues for women and minorities in academia. Two recent reports from the National Research Council (2007, 2010a) discuss the persistence of gender gaps in the professoriate as well as strategies for effectively addressing these gaps. A third report focuses on improving the STEM pipeline for the three separate racial/ethnic categories generally aggregated as "underrepresented minorities": African Americans, American Indians and Alaska Natives, and Latinos/as (National Research Council, 2010b). These important publications highlight how the large-scale demographic changes underway in the United States affect the STEM enterprise and how U.S. diversity can address the challenges of the globalization of science and engineering (National Research Council, 2007, 2010c).

Two National Science Foundation (NSF) programs have been part of the national debates. The Alliances for Graduate Education and the Professoriate (AGEP) was implemented in 1999 to address the persistent pipeline problem for African Americans, American Indian and Alaska Natives, and

This research was supported by a grant from the National Science Foundation, ADVANCE: Partnerships for Adaptation, Implementation and Dissemination, HRD#0820057. The use of NSF data does not imply NSF endorsement of the research, research methods, or conclusions contained in this report.

Hispanics and Latinos/as leading to academic STEM positions. A few years later, in 2001, NSF launched the ADVANCE: Institutional Transformation (IT) program. Both of these programs sought to emphasize institutional transformation, recognizing that individuals within these settings typically have limited means to bring about the structural changes necessary to facilitate broader participation in academia. Between 2001 and 2012, 50 colleges or universities each received funding for up to $3.7 million for five years of work under ADVANCE: IT awards.

Each ADVANCE institution crafted a program to fit its structure and culture. Most programs had similar elements with varied methods of implementation. Because most ADVANCE institutions had few women of color, detecting the issues that might be unique for them was initially difficult. Over the course of the program, as more institutions—and increasingly diverse institutions—received awards, the separate issues for women of color began to emerge. Institutions that were awarded ADVANCE grants in 2003 (commonly called the Second Round) all included programmatic elements that sought to attend to the more pronounced underrepresentation of women of color.

Some notes on terminology are warranted. First, we take the terms *minority* and *of color* to be interchangeable, applying the sociological conceptualization of *minority* to reference a category of people who are in a position that has historical and current disadvantages within the larger society. Second, within the STEM context, the particular situation for Asian Americans is complicated and merits additional work beyond the scope of this chapter. "Native Hawaiians and Pacific Islanders" have historically been included in the "Asians and Pacific Islanders" category, but we have not done so. Issues for these two categories (that is, Asians and Pacific Islanders) differ, with experiences of Native Hawaiians and Pacific Islanders being similar to those for American Indians and Alaska Natives. Representing a tiny portion of the U.S. population (less than 1 percent), issues for Native Hawaiians and Pacific Islanders in STEM have not been extensively studied to date. Finally, we use the term *category* rather than *group* to reflect our understanding of these as demographic entities within which there is much variation.

Given the ADVANCE focus on STEM fields, ADVANCE institutions emphasized data-driven approaches. All ADVANCE awardees were required to collect and report data, which included basic demographic information about faculty; the extent to which important resources were distributed equitably (e.g., salaries, space); the extent to which advancement processes were equitable; and the like. A toolkit was developed by the ADVANCE Indicators Working Group (Frehill, Jeser-Cannavale et al., 2005) to permit greater consistency in data collection and reporting, enabling cross-institutional comparisons. Another toolkit on evaluation was developed to provide ADVANCE awardees with resources to document programmatic impact (Frehill, Batista et al., 2006). Over the years, evaluation needs for the AGEP program drove the development of streamlined methods of data reporting for this program as well (Frehill, 2011).

ADVANCE is a program that spans widely different disciplines, but individual practitioners within those fields often failed to appreciate the ways in which the representation of women across fields and faculty rank differed greatly, assuming that the situation in their own field was generalizable to that for all women in all fields. This fallacy, too, held specific implications for programming that was developed to address issues for women of color. Such programming, therefore, sometimes failed to account for the "double consciousness" (DuBois, 1903; Hill-Collins, 1990) or multiple marginality (Turner, 2002) that women of color might experience within academia.

The need for high-quality, reliable data to enable decision making about faculty and graduate student issues is an important lesson of ADVANCE and AGEP. The NSF's published reports are one place to start. Figures 1.1 and 1.2 illustrate the numerical differences across fields for women and the more pronounced underrepresentation of faculty of color in academia. As shown in Figure 1.1, women's representation is highest in psychology, social sciences, and life sciences and lowest in the physical sciences and engineering. Within all fields, there is an inverse relationship between rank and percentage female. The scarcity of faculty of color is reflected in Figure 1.2, which shows the representation by rank for underrepresented minority and Asian faculty. While these data could be separated by discipline for Asian faculty, the small numbers of other faculty of color meant that much data were suppressed in NSF's reporting.

The data shown in Figures 1.1 and 1.2 related to faculty representation of women and minorities are similar to those that show the "pipeline" into these disciplines via postsecondary education. Data on women's representation across fields and degree levels—bachelor's, master's, and PhD—show that the higher the degree level, the lower the participation of women. In addition, the data show that women are persistently underrepresented in fields such as engineering and computer science, but are entering and moving up the academic ladder in relatively larger numbers in the social sciences and psychology. Similarly, as degree level increases, the relative percentage of underrepresented minorities decreases. Unlike women, who are no longer underrepresented at some levels in some STEM fields, underrepresented minorities lag far behind "parity." African Americans, Latinos/as, and American Indians and Alaska Natives collectively account for 36% of the U.S. 18- to 24-year-old population, yet represented 22% or less of all degrees at all levels awarded in all STEM fields in 2009 (National Action Council for Minorities in Engineering, 2011).

For the AGEP evaluation, there were long-standing issues about data collection by the participating institutions; few personnel at these institutions had experience in this area. Further, there were persistent concerns about the validity of making comparisons of the AGEP participants to other

Figure 1.1. Percent Female Among Doctorate Recipients and Doctoral Faculty at Four-Year Educational Institutions by Rank and Broad Field, 2008

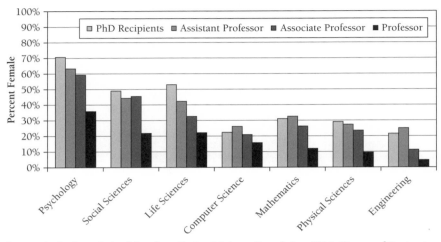

Sources: Author's analysis of data from National Science Foundation, 2012, "Survey of Doctorate Recipients, 2008, Detailed Statistical Tables," and National Science Foundation, 2009, "Doctorate Recipients from U.S. Universities: Summary Report, 2007–08."

Figure 1.2. Percent Men and Women of Color Among Doctorate Recipients and Doctoral Faculty at Four-Year Educational Institutions by Rank, 2008

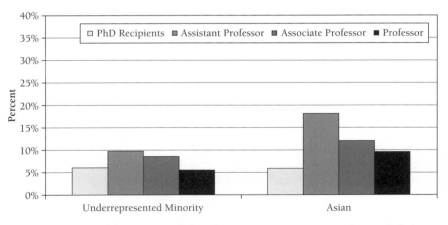

Note: "Underrepresented minority" includes African Americans, American Indians and Alaska Natives, and Hispanics. "Asian" does not include Native Hawaiians or Other Pacific Islanders.
Sources: Author's analysis of data from National Science Foundation, 2012, "Survey of Doctorate Recipients, 2008, Detailed Statistical Tables," and National Science Foundation, 2009, "Doctorate Recipients from U.S. Universities: Summary Report, 2007–08."

groups of students that became entangled with the efforts to collect data on the students' progress in their graduate program. Data collection about women of color was an even greater challenge across the ADVANCE institutions. The relatively small numbers posed confidentiality problems, with each institution handling these data in different ways. Initially, few of the early ADVANCE awardees addressed issues for women of color, but the emphasis on attending to these issues increased with each subsequent ADVANCE cohort. More detailed data at the disciplinary level were necessary: The reports based on NSF data, although they had large sample sizes, were limited when one was interested in drilling down to the finer level of demographic detail associated with the interaction of race/ethnicity and gender, as shown in Figure 1.2.

A promising way to fill this void is through the engagement of professional, discipline-based societies in STEM fields, which collect data on their membership and the status of the respective discipline. In this chapter, we answer several interrelated questions about the potential role of professional societies in programs to improve the participation of women of color in academic STEM: (1) to what extent are data available?; (2) how might these data be provided to such programs in a meaningful and comparable way?; (3) what are the methodological issues associated with collecting and reporting data, especially on small subgroups like women of color?; and (4) to what extent might professional societies, as organizations that facilitate collective action by members in their fields, also be important mechanisms for bringing about demographic change within their fields?

Methods: Collecting Data About Professional Societies

To answer these questions, we began by developing an inventory of data collection and reporting by professional societies based on our knowledge of professional societies as potential resources of data on STEM faculty diversity. Professional societies are potentially an excellent source of data compared with other national data collection efforts. Societies have well-established reputations with the community of professionals in their disciplines. Further, some societies invest resources in the collection and reporting of their own faculty data, often with experts in survey research on their staffs to do so. Results of their surveys can be provided to members quickly, in stark contrast to the slow reporting associated with many other national data collection efforts. In some cases, data collection within professional societies has evolved over time and has become an institutionalized service societies provide to their members. For example, department chairs often compare their own data about number of faculty members and number of degrees granted to similar data from other departments. Professional societies appear to be well trusted by faculty in their disciplines and are considered reliable sources of information.

New Directions for Higher Education • DOI:10.1002/he

In April 2009, we contacted the staffs of 57 professional societies to inquire about data availability on women and minority faculty in their disciplines. The broad fields of these 57 professional societies were: engineering (10), life science (17), health science (4), mathematics and computer science (10), physical science (8), and social science (8). We requested copies of questionnaires and reports. Of the 57 societies we contacted, 38 responded in some way (67% response rate), although not all of the responding societies had questionnaires or reports. Of the responding societies, the majority (25) collected some kind of national data or published reports on women and/or minority faculty members in their disciplines or could derive some such information from their membership databases. We received 14 data reports from professional societies on women of color in science, technology, engineering, and math. The Appendix to this chapter provides links to these 14 reports.

In June 2009, we led a workshop attended by 24 representatives of 18 different professional societies. The workshop's goals were to share information about the inventory and to determine the extent to which STEM societies' existing data collections could provide data on women of color to programs such as AGEP and ADVANCE. We summarized the data collection instruments and methods used by the responding professional societies and distributed copies of instruments. Materials were also made available online after the workshop. We conducted a descriptive analysis of the professional society reports and surveys on STEM faculty. These original analyses were supplemented with a more recent examination of the materials to determine the extent of data collection about graduate students. We compiled information on types of data sources, methodology, and questionnaire content and analyzed the content of the 14 questionnaires to which we had access, including the type of demographic and work-related data collected, such as race, sex, rank, tenure status, and salary.

Findings: Three Types of Data Sources

Table 1.1 shows the three main sources of information about faculty members: membership databases, surveys directed to individual members, and surveys directed to academic departments.

As shown in Table 1.1, six societies offered to provide aggregated membership data, which varied in comparability and availability (some societies considered this information proprietary). Membership data are not generally collected for the purpose of publicly describing faculty members, so they are rarely published. In addition, different questions were used to collect the same information. For example, race was asked in many ways. One of the most common differences was whether Hispanic origin and race were asked together or separately. Employment information was also collected differently. Some societies identified faculty members as those who "work at a university," while others classified them as working "in education." Either way can be problematic, as not all those employed at universities are faculty members,

NEW DIRECTIONS FOR HIGHER EDUCATION • DOI:10.1002/he

Table 1.1. STEM Professional Society Sources of Faculty Data

Willing to Share Membership Data	Surveys of Members	Department Surveys*	
American Institute of Chemical Engineers	Association for Computing Machinery	American Geological Institute	American Sociological Association
American Society of Civil Engineers	Society for Neuroscience	Computing Research Association	American Psychological Association
American Nuclear Society	American Meteorological Society	Consortium for Ocean Leadership	American Political Science Association
Society for Industrial and Applied Math	American Chemical Society	American Statistical Association	American Society for Engineering Education
American Society for Cell Biology		American Institute of Physics	Association of American Medical Colleges
Biophysical Society		American Mathematical Society	American Economic Association
		Conference Board of the Mathematical Sciences (bachelor's departments only)	Committee on the Status of Women and Committee on the Status of Minorities

*Note: All societies that collect faculty data from departments also collect data about graduate students.

and not all those working in education are employed at universities or are members of the faculty. Such problems with comparability applied not just to membership data, but also to survey data collected by professional societies.

Four societies collected data from individual society members. These surveys were not necessarily conducted for the specific purpose of collecting data about faculty. These efforts were typically general membership surveys conducted for a variety of reasons, including assessment of member satisfaction with various membership benefits. However, these questionnaires typically asked about race, gender, and employment, so that even if not published, most societies could (and expressed a willingness to) supply these data on request.

There were limitations on the data collected via questionnaires sent to individuals. Often, there is no list of the population of faculty members in a given discipline. The professional societies instead survey only their members, and such surveys would miss, for example, any chemistry professors who are not members of the American Chemical Society. This problem is exacerbated in interdisciplinary fields, because faculty members who come from a variety of disciplines belong to a variety of professional societies: They may be missed by some questionnaires and counted multiple times through others.

Department chair surveys were the most common type of survey (14 responding professional societies). Paper or electronic survey forms requested department chairs to provide information about their faculty. One advantage of department questionnaires was that the data included professionals who were possibly not society members.

Professional societies collected data from departments in two ways: (1) by asking for aggregated data on the number of faculty members or (2) by asking departments to provide information about individual faculty members. Among the societies listed in Table 1.1, only the American Sociological Association and the American Psychological Association asked department chairs to report demographics anonymously about individual faculty members. The others all asked for aggregated race/ethnicity and sex, often as separate items, with the result that reports included data on faculty sex and race/ethnicity separately, making women of color invisible.

Although the department survey response rates were usually high, accuracy could be an issue with race/ethnicity, as these were reported by department chairs or administrative assistants rather than by individuals themselves. Respondents may not know how to classify someone else or may not know which of the categories provided on the questionnaire apply to certain faculty members. In addition, department surveys asking for individual data on faculty members could present a heavy burden for the respondent.

Survey Methodologies

History and Frequency. Some societies have a long tradition of conducting member surveys, while others have started more recently. For example, the Conference Board of the Mathematical Sciences has been surveying undergraduate mathematics departments since 1965. Surveys that started long ago are unlikely to have data for the entire history of the survey on faculty race and sex. The American Institute of Physics started to survey department chairs about faculty members in 1986, but has collected race and/or gender data for only the last ten years. Most responding societies collected data annually, three collected it less frequently, and all but one were on a regular collection schedule.

Paper Versus Web. Most societies' surveys gave respondents a choice of an online or paper form. This "mixed mode" approach was particularly effective for department-level surveys, because these surveys require the respondent to look through administrative records, which is easier to do with a paper survey. Paper questionnaires also conveyed a sense of importance, as they are increasingly rare in the current age of web-only surveys. The length of questionnaires also varied. Some were as short as two pages, while others were much longer. In particular, surveys that asked department chairs to report individual, rather than aggregated, data about faculty members tended to be longer. Some surveys, too, featured extensive definitions to increase reliability, which increased the length of the questionnaire.

Populations Versus Samples. Somewhat surprisingly, we were unable to find information on whether many of the societies used populations or samples for their data collection. However, membership surveys were generally done on samples. Most of the department surveys for which we had information used the entire population of departments known to the society. Some exceptions included three societies that collected data on only doctorate-granting departments, while the Conference Board of the Mathematical Sciences collected data only from undergraduate departments, including those at two-year colleges.

Questionnaire Length and Response Rates. Most society surveys' response rates exceeded 50% with many higher than 90%. While there is a well-documented relationship between questionnaire organization and response rates (Dillman, 2000), response rates were quite high for the Computing Research Association's lengthy 29-page questionnaire (with its optional pages and meticulous definitions). Society survey researchers were keenly aware of the additional burden that completing a questionnaire imposed on department chairs; they expressed interest in keeping surveys brief and avoiding other changes that could hinder responses. At the heart of these issues were the professional societies' existing relationships and their established reputation of providing useful information back to departments from the surveys. Therefore, the ongoing nature of these surveys meant that societies were reluctant to make instrumentation changes for fear of reducing response rates or negatively impacting comparability over time.

Professional Society Data Reports on Women of Color in STEM

All of the societies from which we received questionnaires collected information on rank, sex, and race/ethnicity of faculty members. As previously discussed, some societies collected data on individual faculty members, while others asked departments to report aggregated information about their faculty members, which limited how data on race/ethnicity and sex could be reported. Most societies collected data on faculty rank and tenure, but only a few collected data on salary.

Several societies collected data on both race and sex of faculty members. These societies could provide data on women faculty members of color upon request; however, their data on women of color had not yet been published:

- American Society for Engineering Education
- American Chemical Society
- American Statistical Association
- American Psychological Association
- American Sociological Association

We found only three societies with published reports that included data on faculty women of color:

- Association of American Medical Colleges (Leadley, Magrane, Lang, & Pham, 2009)
- Conference Board of the Mathematical Sciences (Lutzer, Rodi, Kirkman, & Maxwell, 2007)
- American Institute of Physics (Ivie, 2010)

Each of these reports presented the data in different formats, with Association of American Medical Colleges reporting numbers of faculty, the American Institute of Physics reporting numbers of women, and Conference Board of the Mathematical Sciences reporting percentages. All are valuable resources for benchmarking women faculty members of color in mathematics, physics, and academic medicine and can serve as exemplars for other societies. Analyses of the membership databases and surveys noted in Table 1.1 could use statistical methods to derive disaggregated data on women of color if the sample sizes were sufficient.

Collecting data on the very small number of minorities in STEM professional societies, particularly women of color, was one of the foremost challenges faced by data collectors. In some fields, the number of women faculty in some racial-ethnic categories is so small (fewer than five) that it tested the limits of standard collection and reporting methods. There was much controversy stirred when NSF's Science Resource Statistics division (now the National Center for Science and Engineering Statistics) changed its annual report on the Survey of Earned Doctorates (Mervis, 2009; Plewes, 2010). The suppression of small cells and changes in aggregation caused a public outcry among those who were advocates of broadening participation of underrepresented groups in STEM fields and among those who had been tracking these data over many years.

Society data collectors also faced confidentiality issues. Small numbers frequently posed challenges associated with instrumentation. The simplicity of a questionnaire was often associated with a high response rate; therefore, the added complexity associated with collecting data in which some cells were likely to be empty may increase the completion time—with very little perceived overall benefit—while threatening response rates. While there is some merit to showing "zero" cells to call attention to a potential demographic problem (Nelson & Brammer, 2010), department chairs completing surveys may not share this view.

In spite of such concerns, the American Institute of Physics (AIP) published the number of women faculty of color in physics departments. This decision was based partly on feedback from the physics community, some of whom felt that it was important to publicize the small numbers in hopes of increasing them. Also, some women scientists of color have reported to AIP that they do not mind potentially being identified, because their ethnicity and sex are hardly secrets (that is, they are already visible).

Conclusions and Recommendations

Despite changes in the legal structures of discrimination, the professoriate in STEM fields at U.S. academic institutions continues to be dominated by White males. In short, the U.S. population is becoming more diverse with more pronounced heterogeneity in younger than in older generations, but the professoriate has been slow to change.

Will academic institutions be able to effectively tap this pool of talent, and to what extent does the professoriate resemble the nation? Figures 1.1 and 1.2 showed that the professoriate, especially in the highest, most powerful full-professor rank, continues to be largely White and male. According to the National Science Foundation (2009), 67% of all doctoral-degreed STEM faculty at four-year universities are men, and 78% are non-Hispanic White (men and women: the 2006 data are not disaggregated by gender and race/ ethnicity simultaneously). Modeling the process they term "demographic inertia," Hargens and Long (2002) show that even in a field where women comprise half of those graduating with doctoral degrees, it would take 35 years—a career-span—for a discipline to reach half women across academic ranks, given the rates of faculty attrition and replacement. Marschke, Laursen, Nielsen, and Rankin (2007) show that with careful interventions, such as the ones that many ADVANCE institutions have implemented, this process can be quickened so that gender equity among the professoriate can be increased sooner.

NEW DIRECTIONS FOR HIGHER EDUCATION • DOI:10.1002/he

Professional societies have the potential to be valuable resources to their members and to institutions trying to measure progress in the recruitment and retention of women faculty of color. Customarily, high response rates and a view of survey results as a member benefit mean that professionals generally trust society data. Further, the rapid reporting-back to their constituents means that the professional society data are timelier than those analyzed and published by government organizations like NSF. However, while many professional societies collect their own data via surveys or are willing to make available data from membership databases, we found that only eight collected data on both race and sex of faculty, which is necessary for reporting on women of color. Of these eight, only three have published reports including data on women of color as of the date of our research.

There are challenges in data comparability across disciplines due to differences in question wording and reporting formats. It is unclear how effective an effort to make data more comparable would be, or the extent to which this would be a critical part of the effort to communicate relevant national-level data to funding agencies. Societies' bureaucratic and governance structures may make it difficult to change questionnaires and reporting. The benefits of adopting new measures and formats have to be convincing to justify this loss of internal comparability.

Because of low minority representation, data collectors continue to struggle with the confidentiality issues associated with small numbers. Given the centrality of this issue on a national level (for example, see Plewes, 2010), these and related issues need to be carefully considered and advice should be provided to the professional societies. A prominent nonsocial scientist working without institutional review board (IRB) supervision has reported the small numbers at research universities, in what she calls a story of "ones and zeroes," as illustrative (Nelson & Brammer, 2010). Such reporting "freedom" is not permitted to social scientists, whose research is carefully overseen by IRBs. Even when IRB issues are not salient for professional societies, the ethical issues associated with reporting small numbers continue to pose challenges to social scientists who are concerned about confidentiality.

Much of the research on women of color in STEM fields has been completed for theses and dissertations that focus on a specific institution or small set of institutions and very small sample sizes. Hence, much of this research has not been published in more widely read peer-review publications (M. Ong, personal communication, March 18, 2010). In reference to her work with Orfield that synthesized 115 empirical studies of women of color in STEM, Ong has indicated that these findings are often invisible to larger audiences (Ong, Wright, Espinosa, & Orfield, 2011). While professional society data are distributed to the discipline-specific communities they serve, most professional societies lack the mechanism to distribute their data to cross-disciplinary audiences.

Professional societies need more information on how their data can benefit institutions and about programmatic efforts to expand underrepresented groups' participation in the professoriate. In light of these findings, we recommend that college administrators and professional societies work together to address gaps in data collection and reporting. Often the lack of reporting on such small populations results in an assumption that there are no women of color. By encouraging professional societies to report on existing data or supplement ongoing data collection and reporting, progress for women of color in the professoriate can be made more visible.

References

Dillman, D. (2000). *Mail and Internet surveys: The tailored design method* (2nd ed). New York, NY: John Wiley & Sons.

DuBois, W. E. B. (1903). *The souls of Black folk.* Chicago, IL: McClurg and Co.

Frehill, L. (2011). Reporting formats. In Y. George, S. Malcom, & P. Campbell (Eds.), *Measuring diversity: An evaluation guide for STEM graduate school leaders* (pp. 41–48). Washington, DC: American Association for the Advancement of Science.

Frehill, L., Batista, E., Edwards Lange, S., Gonzalez-Baker, S., Jeser-Cannavale, C., Malley, J. ... Sviglin, H. (2006). *Using program evaluation to ensure the success of your ADVANCE program.* Retrieved from http://wiseli.engr.wisc.edu/docs/Report_Tool kit2_2006.pdf

Frehill, L., Jeser-Cannavale, C., Kehoe, P., Meader, E., Sheridan, J., Stewart, A., & Sviglin, H. (2005). *Toolkit for reporting progress toward NSF ADVANCE: Institutional transformation goals.* Retrieved from www.advance.vt.edu/documents/other/advance _indicators_toolkit.pdf

Hargens, L. L., & Long, J. S. (2002). Demographic inertia and women's representation among faculty in higher education. *Journal of Higher Education, 73*(4), 494–517.

Hill-Collins, P. (1990). *Black feminist thought: Knowledge, consciousness, and the politics of empowerment.* New York, NY: Routledge.

Ivie, R. (2010). Women of color in physics departments: A data snapshot. *Committee for the Status of Women in Physics Gazette, 29*(1). Retrieved from www.aps.org/programs /women/reports/gazette/loader.cfm?csModule=security/getfile&PageID=205973

Leadley, J., Magrane, D., Lang, J., & Pham, T. (2009). *Women in U.S. academic medicine statistics and benchmarking report, 2007–08.* Association of American Medical Colleges. Retrieved from www.aamc.org/download/53434/data/wimstats_2008.pdf

Lutzer, D. J., Rodi, S., Kirkman, E., & Maxwell, J. (2007). *Statistical abstract of undergraduate programs in the mathematical sciences in the United States: Fall 2005 CBMS survey.* Retrieved from www.ams.org/profession/data/cbms-survey/chapter4.pdf

Marschke, R., Laursen, S., Nielsen, J., & Rankin, R. (2007). Demographic inertia revisited: An immodest proposal to achieve equitable gender representation among faculty in higher education. *Journal of Higher Education, 78*(1), 1–26.

Mervis, J. (2009). NSF restores data on minority PhDs. *Science, 323,* 1161.

National Action Council for Minorities in Engineering. (2011). *The 2011 NACME data book.* White Plains, NY: Author.

National Research Council. (2007). *Beyond bias and barriers: Fulfilling the potential of women in academic science and engineering.* Washington, DC: National Academies Press.

National Research Council. (2010a). *Gender differences at critical transitions in the careers of science, engineering, and mathematics faculty.* Washington, DC: National Academies Press.

National Research Council. (2010b). *Expanding underrepresented minority participation: America's science and technology talent at the crossroads.* Washington, DC: National Academies Press.

National Research Council. (2010c). *Rising above the gathering storm, revisited: Rapidly approaching Category 5.* Washington, DC: National Academies Press.

National Science Foundation. (2009). *Characteristics of doctoral scientists and engineers in the United States: 2006 detailed statistical tables NSF 09-317.* Project Officer, D. J. Foley. Arlington, VA: Author.

National Science Foundation. (2012). *Doctorate recipients from US universities.* Retrieved from http://www.nsf.gov/statistics/sed/digest/2011/nsf13301.pdf

Nelson, D., & Brammer, C. (2010). *A national analysis of minorities in science and engineering faculties at research universities.* Retrieved from http://faculty-staff.ou.edu/N/Donna.J.Nelson-1/diversity/Faculty_Tables_FY07/07Report.pdf

Ong, M., Wright, C., Espinosa, L., & Orfield, G. (2011). Inside the double bind. *Harvard Educational Review, 81*(2), 172–209.

Plewes, T. (2010). *Protecting and accessing data from the Survey of Earned Doctorates: A workshop summary.* Washington, DC: National Academies Press.

Turner, C. (2002). Women of color in academe: Living with multiple marginality. *Journal of Higher Education, 73*(1), 74–93.

LISA M. FREHILL *is a senior analyst at Energetics Technology Center in Waldorf, MD.*

RACHEL IVIE *is associate director of the Statistical Research Center at the American Institute of Physics.*

NEW DIRECTIONS FOR HIGHER EDUCATION • DOI:10.1002/he

APPENDIX

Professional Society Data Reports on Women of Color in Science, Technology, Engineering, and Math

American Sociological Association
www.asanet.org/research/index.cfm

Association of American Medical Colleges
www.aamc.org/members/gwims/statistics/

American Physiological Society
www.the-aps.org/mm/Education/Publications/Education-Reports/Diversity

American Mathematical Society
www.ams.org/employment/deptprof.html

Conference Board of the Mathematical Sciences
www.ams.org/cbms/

American Psychological Association
www.apa.org/workforce/about/index.aspx

Computing Research Association
www.cra.org/statistics/

American Society for Engineering Education
www.asee.org/papers-and-publications/publications/college-profiles

American Geological Institute
www.agiweb.org/workforce/reports.html

American Political Science Association
www.apsanet.org/content_7589.cfm

American Institute of Physics
www.aip.org/statistics/

American Statistical Association
www.amstat.org/education/departmentsurveys.cfm

Committee on the Status of Women in the Economic Profession
www.cswep.org/annual_reports.htm

Committee on the Status of Minority Groups in the Economics Profession
www.aeaweb.org/committees/CSMGEP/reports/

2

Career development programs for graduate students should acknowledge the multiple and often conflicting demands placed on underrepresented scholars.

From Graduate School to the STEM Workforce: An Entropic Approach to Career Identity Development for STEM Women of Color

Kelly Mack, Claudia Rankins, Kamilah Woodson

Improved global economies and opportunities no longer allow the United States to rely on foreign-born talent to meet STEM workforce demands. If the United States is to remain a competitive leader in science and engineering, radically different approaches to increase and better prepare future generations of U.S.-born scientists and engineers for global competition are imperative. However, the current representation of minority women (i.e., Black, Hispanic, and American Indian) in these disciplines is less than one-third of their representation in the U.S. populace. According to the most recent U.S. Census Bureau statistics, minority women comprise 14.3% of the U.S. population. Between the ages of 18–24 and 25–64, this percentage increases to 17.5% and 15.9%, respectively. This community not only represents a significant part of what is expected to become the largest percentage of U.S. population by the year 2042 (U.S. Census Bureau, 2008) but also represents the rich source of talent required for the United States to remain a global leader.

In its recent report, *Engaging to Excel*, the President's Council of Advisors on Science and Technology (PCAST; 2012) noted that the United States requires one million more STEM baccalaureates in the next decade. Critically important to attaining the PCAST goal is the need to broaden the participation of underrepresented groups, particularly women of color, who more than their White counterparts indicate an interest in pursuing baccalaureate study in STEM disciplines. According to recent data from the National Science Foundation (NSF), 32.3% of women of color who were

NEW DIRECTIONS FOR HIGHER EDUCATION, no. 163, Fall 2013   © Wiley Periodicals, Inc.
Published online in Wiley Online Library (wileyonlinelibrary.com) • DOI:10.1002/he.20062

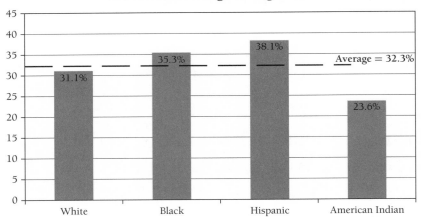

Figure 2.1. Intentions of Women Freshmen to Major in Science and Engineering Fields

freshmen in college in 2010 noted intentions to major in science and engineering fields, while only 31.3% of their White counterparts indicated the same (National Science Foundation, 2011; Figure 2.1). These data support current literature that dispels myths attributing lack of interest to the low representation of women of color in STEM disciplines (Ong, Wright, Espinosa, & Orfield, 2011).

Despite the heightened interest of women of color when entering science and engineering fields at the baccalaureate level, there exists a steadily declining rate of retention in these disciplines at all academic levels. Collectively, women of color make up only 10.6% of all of the recipients of bachelor's degrees in the STEM disciplines in the United States. This percentage falls precipitously to 5.4% at the doctoral level. Even in fields such as the biological sciences and psychology, where college women of color are either at or near parity with their U.S. representation, such is not the case at the doctoral level where they are underrepresented by as much as 11.3% and 3.9%, respectively (Table 2.1). Similarly, in other STEM disciplines where women are wholly underrepresented, such as the computer sciences, women of color earn 6.6% of the bachelor's degrees, but only 0.5% of the doctoral degrees in these disciplines.

At the faculty levels, a similar trend is observed. U.S.-born, underrepresented minority women comprise only 3.6%, 2.5%, and 1.2% of all assistant, associate, and full professors, respectively, in the STEM disciplines. It is important to note that while there is persistent and pervasive attrition from the STEM disciplines for all women of color, further empirical analysis reveals important differences among subpopulations of women of color that are important in informing current and future strategies for retention. Table 2.2 indicates the change in percent of women of color in the STEM

NEW DIRECTIONS FOR HIGHER EDUCATION • DOI:10.1002/he

Table 2.1. Percentage and Number of Women Science and Engineering Baccalaureate Degrees and PhDs, by Discipline and Race/Ethnicity

		BS			PhD		
		Black	Hisp	Am Ind	Black	Hisp	Am Ind
Biological Science	%	5.4	4.5	0.4	1.4	1.6	0.03
	#	3969	3247	318	91	108	2
Computer Science	%	4.4	1.6	0.1	0.3	0.2	0
	#	1892	697	66	4	3	0
Earth Science	%	0.8	1.8	0.4	0.3	1.5	0
	#	30	70	15	2	11	0
Engineering	%	1.4	1.7	0.1	0.6	0.5	0
	#	979	1166	71	42	33	0
Physics	%	1.1	1	0.1	0.1	0.1	0
	#	49	48	5	2	2	0
Psychology	%	8.4	7.2	0.5	4.3	4.8	0.3
	#	7415	6385	464	141	157	12

Source: National Science Foundation, 2009.

Table 2.2. Percentage of Women of Color in Science and Engineering, 2006

					Faculty %		
	BS %	(BS–PhD)	PhD %	(PhD– Faculty)	Asst Prof	Assoc Prof	Full Prof
Black	5.9	55.9%	2.6	26.9%	1.9	1.2	0.7
Hispanic	4.3	39.5%	2.6	42.3%	1.5	1.1	0.4
American Indian	0.4	50.0%	0.2	0.0%	0.2	0.2	0.1

Source: National Science Foundation, 2009.

disciplines between the bachelor's, doctoral, and faculty levels. The greatest change for African American and American Indian women occurs between the bachelor's and doctoral degree levels at 55.9% and 50%, respectively. This change suggests that efforts targeting entry into and persistence through graduate-degree programs will yield the most optimal results for women from these underrepresented groups. On the other hand, the greatest percent change in representation for Hispanic women exists between the graduate and faculty levels, suggesting that efforts targeting their entry into the professoriate would yield the most optimal results.

Overall, the common target area of focus for increasing the representation of women of color in STEM disciplines lies at either entry into or exit from graduate school. However, aside from identifying appropriate academic targets of intervention, it is critical that such interventions be informed by accurate and precise details that fully define the exact numbers of women of color required, by discipline, to reach parity. As outlined in

NEW DIRECTIONS FOR HIGHER EDUCATION • DOI:10.1002/he

Table 2.3. Number of Science and Engineering PhDs Needed to Reach Parity

	Biological Sciences	Computer Sciences	Earth Sciences	Engineering	Physics	Psychology
Black	468	96	48	504	144	236
Hispanic	554	123	60	541	164	268
American Indian	33	7	4	36	7	17

Table 2.3, based on the current representation of women of color in the U.S. population (U.S. Census Bureau, 2008) and the number of earned doctorates awarded in STEM disciplines (National Science Foundation, 2009), it would be necessary for the United States to produce a total of 2,375 additional women of color doctorates. This seems a plausible goal, given the relatively robust pool of women of color at the bachelor's degree level.

However, the disaggregated data needed to inform the nation's trajectory toward equity in STEM for women of color are not available beyond 2006. This deficit significantly hampers the capacity of the academy to effectively redress current trends for women of color. Further, there is comparatively little reported in the literature that either explains the disparate representation of women of color in STEM fields or elucidates the potential areas for successful intervention. Recently, Ong and colleagues (2011) reported that, among thousands of published works on underrepresented minorities in STEM fields, there are fewer than 200 works of scholarship that specifically seek to provide insight on the factors that influence the retention, persistence, and achievement of women of color in those same fields. Within the scholarship that does exist, widely accepted reasons to explain low levels of representation of women of color include a persistent lack of role models. Recent studies suggest that one of the greatest influences and determinants of success in STEM disciplines for women students is access to same-gender role models (Bettinger & Long, 2005). Additionally, O'Neill (2002) reports that same-gender and same-race mentoring for minorities is often characterized by stronger psychosocial support and, therefore, may yield better career outcomes. However, while underrepresented minority women continue to comprise an increasingly significant percentage of the student population in the science and engineering disciplines, current levels of women faculty of color are far below the level of critical mass and, therefore, are too few in number to provide underrepresented minority women students with sufficient access to preferred role models (Etzkowitz, Kemelgor, Neuschatz, Uzzi, & Alonzo, 2002).

In addition to a lack of access to culturally sensitive role models, women of color unduly experience limited access to mentoring, which could provide essential tools for negotiating success in the academy (Evans & Cokley, 2008; Jordan-Zachary, 2004). However, culturally competent

NEW DIRECTIONS FOR HIGHER EDUCATION • DOI:10.1002/he

mentoring, exclusively designed to provide a context that is appropriately rooted in and relevant to minority population cultures, is oftentimes under-employed (Evans & Cokley, 2008; Jordan, 2006; Mack, Rankins, & Allen, 2009). The blended integration of the components of culturally competent mentoring (focusing on cultural complexities, demonstrating an awareness of social pressures and influences, and emphasizing personal connected-ness) is not only successful in retaining underrepresented minority stu-dents in the STEM disciplines and contributing to their persistence toward science careers (Evans & Cokley, 2008; Jordan, 2006; Mack & Taylor, 2008; Mack et al., 2009), but could also be equally as effective in address-ing the underrepresentation of women faculty of color in the STEM disciplines.

Concomitant to intrinsic barriers to advancement for women of color within the academy are societal imbalances that are extrinsic to the acad-emy, yet distinctively experienced by women of color. In 1975, participants of the Double Bind Conference of Minority Women Scientists noted chal-lenges related to strong, traditional gender roles that are highly characteris-tic of minority communities and result in increased domestic responsibility and related familial stressors (Malcom, Hall, & Brown, 1976). Similarly, the literature for underrepresented minority women documents the dispropor-tionate burden of adverse health conditions and outcomes as well as mini-mized access to aggressive medical approaches to treatment and preventative health care (Satcher, 2001; Shavers, 2007).

While these influences do not fully encompass the entirety of the unique disposition of women of color in the academic STEM disciplines, they do contribute to their persistently low representation in meaningful ways. Institutions of higher education and scientific societies have made Herculean attempts to address the underrepresentation of women of color in the STEM fields at all educational and academic professional levels, but with minimal success. It is believed that the low level of success is due, either wholly or in part, to the absence of a comprehensive approach. Reli-ance upon granular levels of evaluation and analysis as well as consider-ation for the sociocultural burdens of women of color in the United States proves necessary. Such approaches would afford the STEM fields increased capacity to customize interventions appropriately. In the current formative model for career identity development, we focus on a national, inclusive, and multipronged working strategy toward empowering academic STEM women of color in the academy. This model influences the full integration of women of color, while also raising the national level of consciousness about this special population in the academy. This holistic approach, rooted in social and physical sciences, serves as the foundation upon which additional efforts targeting all women of color, regardless of aca-demic level, can be mirrored and tailored as appropriate for maximal impact.

Entropic Career Identity Development (EnCID) Model

Many scholars have developed theories that explain career development and all of its complexities. One such theory is the Social Cognitive Career Theory (SCCT), which offers three segmental yet interlocking process models of career development (Lent, 2005; Lent, Brown, & Hackett, 2002; Leung, 2008). This theory emphasizes that self-efficacy and career expectations are shaped by various learning experiences (Lent, 2005; Lent et al., 2002; Leung, 2008). However, though widely accepted and adapted, SCCT and similar career choice and development theories have only minimally been made applicable to underrepresented groups in general (Brown, 2002). Specifically for women of color, these theories also fail to enhance understanding of the inextricably linked roles of gender and race and their impact on career actualization (Lent et al., 2002). These limitations, coupled with the intrinsic and extrinsic pressures of the academy for women of color, suggest that there is overwhelming need for career development models that are dynamic and keenly sensitive to the cultural identity development of women of color in STEM academic and professional contexts.

Unlike career development models and theories, identity development models account for both gender and culture within the context of identity development. The Nigrescence Racial Identity Development Model (Cross, 1971) and the Womanist Identity Development Model (Helms, 1990), for example, have similar frameworks that describe the process of transforming from a preexisting identity to one that is crystallized and all-encompassing. The transformation process, divided into four phases, is uniquely targeted to women and provides a fluid structure for describing overall identity development for women of color.

However, to date, no theory exists that fully describes the career or identity development of women of color as they relate to the uniqueness of the academic STEM disciplines. Development of such a theory is believed to require both a reliance on previously developed models and theories (Cross, 1971; Helms, 1990; Lent, 2005; Lent et al., 2002; Leung, 2008) as well as targeted interventions. To that end, the Entropic Career Identity Development (EnCID) Model (Figure 2.2) provides a formative and multidisciplinary framework that holistically considers the intersectionality of multiple identities of women of color, and describes an energized process of career actualization.

Entropy, defined as the tendency for all matter and energy in the universe to evolve toward a state of inert uniformity, serves as the guiding principle that best explains how the career actualization and full integration of women of color in the U.S. STEM enterprise can be achieved. It is important to note that factors contributing to career and self-actualization are developed over time during various phases of identity development. However, it is believed that identity can be achieved sooner and more effectively through a catalytic intervention that is both holistic and targeted. Just

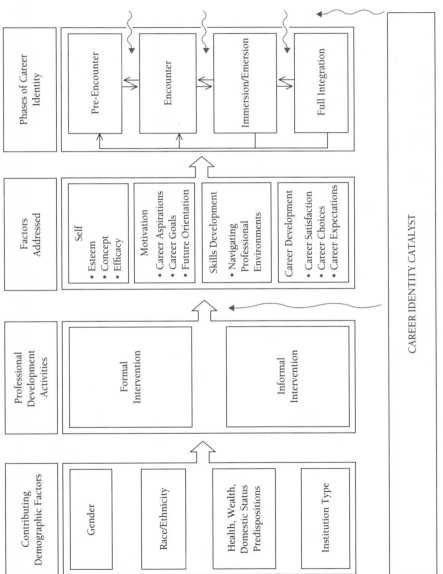

Figure 2.2. Entropic Career Identity Development Model

as molecules in a cold room will mix with molecules in an adjoining warmer room until the temperature in both rooms is uniform, the EnCID molecule suggests that women of color can reach parity with their White and male counterparts, resulting in a heterogeneous academic STEM workforce. Additionally, as depicted in the EnCID model, with appropriate intentional perturbations to the system, such as creating additional openings between the two rooms to enhance the rate of uniformity in temperature, so, too, can catalytic interventions for STEM women of color result, with greater expediency, in their full integration at all academic levels of STEM fields.

The EnCID model assumes that women faculty of color come to academic environments having had a variety of life experiences as well as varying predispositions and levels of exposure to different types of both formal and informal interventions. As a result, it is expected that self-identity, motivation, skills development, and career advancement are enhanced. Subsequently, full career integration is achieved with successful transition through the four phases of development.

The pre-encounter phase of the EnCID model is characterized as a pre-discovery phase of career identity in which the academy is viewed as equitable and the implications of being a woman of color are likely not completely realized. During the second, or encounter, phase of career identity, women of color experience discriminatory incidents that challenge their collective racial and gender identities as well as their academic identities. Such experiences can alter the interpretation of the overall condition of women of color in the academy. During the immersion/emersion phase, women of color are acutely aware of difference and embracing of self; however, the commitment to a healthy identity and view of others is yet to be achieved. Finally, at the level of full integration, women of color not only embrace the intersections of their multiple identities, but also commit to work in the academy in accordance with a newly developed self-image (Cross, 1991; Marks, Settles, Cooke, Morgan, & Sellers, 2004).

While full integration for women of color can be achieved with conventional strategies and interventions, the rate of success is often outpaced by global technological advances, threats to economic stability, and an ever-increasing need to develop and diversify a competitively trained workforce. Thus, the STEM Women of Color Conclave, grounded in the EnCID Model, exists as the quintessential catalyst for fully integrating women of color in the STEM fields and achieving STEM career identity, specifically at the faculty level.

Women faculty of color have long had an impact on the education of women students, particularly from underrepresented minority populations (Mack, Rankins, & Winston, 2011; Wenglinsky, 1996; Wolf-Wendel, 1998). However, the representation of women of color at these levels in the academy is far below that needed to adequately provide underrepresented minority graduate students with sufficient access to either psychosocial support (O'Neill, 2002) or preferred role models (Etzkowitz et al., 2002). Therefore, despite the overwhelming empirical evidence that suggests that interventions are needed at the graduate school level, the Conclave, now in its third year, features a major national convening of women faculty of color from diverse STEM disciplines and professions, as well as nationally recognized leaders with noted scientific expertise related to the study of women of color.

The focus of the Conclave is to form the collective intelligence necessary for building a national network, harness a centralized body of knowledge and best practices related to women of color, and holistically promote (through the phases of career identity) the personal and professional development of women of color in the academy. Also unique to this catalytic component of career identity development is keen attention toward achieving career actualization through the strategic exposure of STEM women of color to the most current social science theory that examines and explains their unique circumstance in the academy and simultaneously supports and accelerates transition through the various stages of career identity.

Because of the matchless relationship between women faculty of color and graduate students, this approach ultimately not only serves to enhance the retention of women faculty of color, but also directly impacts the academic well-being and full integration of women of color at the graduate student level. Further, this highly replicable approach can be tailored to suit the needs of any subpopulation of women of color at either the graduate or undergraduate student levels.

Conclusion

It has been noted that academy and society meetings fulfill many roles for members, including catalyzing and promoting membership culture as well as providing opportunities for the development of professional identity, peer learning, and the establishment of traditions (Frankel & Bird, 2003; Tan & Subramaniam, 2009). Similarly, the Conclave strategy catalyzes, for women of color, the development of a professional network, enhanced visibility, and full integration into the academic STEM fields.

However, Malcom, Hall, and Brown (1976) warn that sporadic attempts to address the underrepresentation of women of color are insufficient and likely to be unsustainable. Hence, the STEM Conclave for Women of Color, rooted in social and physical constructs, also comprises career-identity frameworks that both formatively and formally link it to mainstream analyses. As such, issues uniquely relevant to the intersections of gender and race are conveyed by and highlighted in traditional social science and higher education research. Ultimately, this focus provides for deeper analysis and more specialized efforts that directly target subpopulations of women of color at all STEM academic levels. Such an approach also improves the likelihood for replicability for those audiences, such as women of color graduate students, who can most readily benefit from an energized process to career actualization.

Acknowledgments

The authors wish to acknowledge the Directorate for Education and Human Resources for funding of the Collaborative Career Advancement Project. The authors also wish to acknowledge the following: Dr. Wanda Ward for her visionary leadership; Drs. Lenell Allen and Monya Ruffin for their assistance with the inaugural STEM Women of Color Conclave; Ms. Carmen Rivera for her leadership in Conclave planning and logistics; Dr. Susan Overton; Dr. CoSandra McNeal; Dr. Jasna Jovanovic; and Ms. Danielle Kittrell. Finally, the authors acknowledge the efforts of the initial Conclave Advisory Board: Dr. Yolanda George, Assistant Deputy Director, American Association for the Advancement of Science; Ms. Janet Koster, Executive Director, Association for Women in Science; and Dr. Maria (Mia) Ong, TERC.

References

Bettinger, E., & Long, B. (2005). Do faculty serve as role models? The impact of instructor gender on female students. *American Economic Review, 92*(2), 152–157.

Brown, D. (2002). Introduction to theories of career development and choice: Origins, evolution and current efforts. In D. Brown (Ed.), *Career Choice and Development* (pp. 2–23). San Francisco, CA: Jossey-Bass.

Cross, W. E., Jr. (1971). Toward a psychology of Black liberation: The Negro-to-Black conversion experience. *Black World, 20*(9), 13–27.

Cross, W. E., Jr. (1991). *Shades of black: Diversity in African American identity*. Philadelphia, PA: Temple University Press.

Etzkowitz, H., Kemelgor, C., Neuschatz, M., Uzzi, B., & Alonzo, J. (2002). The paradox of critical mass for women in science. *Science, 266*(5182), 51–54.

Evans, G., & Cokley, K. (2008). African American women and the academy: Using career mentoring to increase research productivity. *Training and Education in Professional Psychology, 2*(1), 50–57.

Frankel, M., & Bird, S. (2003). The role of scientific societies in promoting research integrity. *Science and Engineering Ethics, 9*, 139–140.

Helms, J. E. (1990). *Black and White racial identity: Theory, research, and practice*. Westport, CT: Greenwood Press.

Jordan, D. (2006). *Sisters in science: Conversations with Black women scientists on race, gender, and their passion for science*. West Lafayette, IN: Purdue University Press.

Jordan-Zachary, J. (2004). Reflections on mentoring: Black women and the academy. *Political Science and Politics, 37*(4), 875–877.

Lent, R. (2005). A social cognitive view of career development and counseling. In S. Brown & R. Lent (Eds.), *Career development and counseling: Putting theory and research to work* (pp. 101–127). Hoboken, NJ: John Wiley & Sons, Inc.

Lent, R., Brown, S., & Hackett, G. (2002). *Social cognitive theory in career choice and development* (4th ed.). San Francisco, CA: Jossey-Bass Publishers.

Leung, S. A. (2008). The big-five career theories. In J. Athanasou & R. Esbroeck (Eds.), *International handbook of career guidance* (pp. 115–132). New York, NY: Springer.

Mack, K., Rankins, C., & Allen, L. (2009, May). *Broadening participation for women of color in the academy.* Paper presented at the 3rd Annual Conference on Understanding Interventions that Broaden Participation in Research Careers, Bethesda, MD.

Mack, K., Rankins, C., & Winston, C. (2011). Black women faculty at historically Black colleges and universities: Perspectives for a national imperative. In H. Frierson & W. Tate (Eds.), *Beyond stock stories and folktales: African Americans' paths to STEM fields* (pp. 149–164). Bingley, England: Emerald Group Publishing Limited.

Mack, K., & Taylor, O. (2008, July). *Linking undergraduate and graduate education: A model for enhancing inclusion and participation through the PhD.* Paper presented at the 17th European Access Network (EAN) Annual Conference—Crossing Borders: Diversity in Higher Education, Amsterdam, The Netherlands.

Malcom, S., Hall, P., & Brown, J. (1976). *The double bind: The price of being a minority woman in science.* Washington, DC: American Association for the Advancement of Science.

Marks, B., Settles, I. H., Cooke, D. Y., Morgan, L., & Sellers, R. M. (2004). African American racial-identity: A review of contemporary models and measures. In R. L. Jones (Ed.), *Black psychology* (4th ed., pp. 383–404). Hampton, VA: Cobb & Henry.

National Science Foundation. (2009). *Women, minorities, and persons with disabilities in science and engineering: 2009.* Arlington, VA: Author.

National Science Foundation. (2011). *Women, minorities, and persons with disabilities in science and engineering: 2011.* Arlington, VA: Author.

O'Neill, R. M. (2002). *Mentoring and diversity, an international perspective: Gender and race in mentoring relationships: A review of the literature.* Woburn, MA: Butterworth-Heinemann.

Ong, M., Wright, C., Espinosa, L., & Orfield, G. (2011). Inside the double bind: A synthesis of empirical research on women of color in science, technology, engineering, and mathematics. *Harvard Educational Review, 81*(2), 172–209.

President's Council of Advisors on Science and Technology. (2012). *Engage to excel: Producing one million additional college graduates with degrees in science, technology, engineering, and mathematics.* Retrieved from www.whitehouse.gov/sites/default/files/microsites/ostp/pcast-engage-to-excel-final_2-25-12.pdf

Satcher, D. (2001). Our commitment to eliminate racial and ethnic health disparities. *Yale Journal of Health Policy Law and Ethics, 1,* 1–14.

Shavers, V. (2007). Measurement of socioeconomic status in health disparities research. *Journal of the National Medical Association, 99*(9), 1013–1023.

Tan, L., & Subramaniam, R. (2009). Scientific academies and scientific societies as agents for promoting science culture in developing countries. *International Journal of Technology Management, 46*(1–2), 132–145.

U.S. Census Bureau. (2008). *An older and more diverse nation by midcentury.* Retrieved from www.census.gov/newsroom/releases/archives/population/cb08-123.html

Wenglinsky, H. (1996). The educational justification of historically Black colleges and universities: A policy response to the U.S. Supreme Court. *Educational Evaluation and Policy Analysis, 18*(1), 91–103.

Wolf-Wendel, L. (1998). The baccalaureate origins of successful European American women, African American women, and Latinas. *Journal of Higher Education, 69*(2), 141–186.

KELLY MACK *is executive director of the Association of American College and Universities' Project Kaleidoscope.*

CLAUDIA RANKINS *is a program officer in the Directorate for Education and Human Resources and in the Directorate for Mathematical and Physical Sciences at the National Science Foundation.*

KAMILAH WOODSON *is associate professor of counseling psychology and coordinator of the Doctoral Program in Counseling Psychology at Howard University.*

NEW DIRECTIONS FOR HIGHER EDUCATION • DOI:10.1002/he

3

Latina students who enter higher education and aspire to graduate degrees encounter numerous obstacles along the academic pipeline that ultimately shape their graduate school perspectives.

Motivating Latina Doctoral Students in STEM Disciplines

Elsa C. Ruiz

The current national demographic reality has directed the nation's attention to encouraging and supporting the education of Latinas/os in science, technology, engineering, and mathematics (STEM) disciplines. While increasing the number of minorities in STEM fields has become a national goal and a priority of the Obama administration, less attention has been directed at the specific role mathematics plays in addressing the issue. On a larger scale, research also focuses on the education of Latinas and the need to reduce the achievement gap that persists between them and their White, non-minority, and more affluent counterparts. Gándara and Contreras (2009) note that if action is not taken to prepare this large group of students for college-level coursework, such students run the risk of declining per capita earnings. This chapter focuses on how effective teaching pedagogies can address the obstacles faced by Latina students in the STEM disciplines.

Given the current crisis, the demographic realities, and the present national attention on increasing the number of students in the STEM disciplines, particularly minority and female students, university systems must consider factors that motivate and encourage Latinas on their paths to graduate degrees and eventually to successful STEM careers. Focusing on mathematics education is one way to address this challenge. In this chapter, I examine issues I observed as a mathematics high school teacher, issues that influenced the motivation of all students learning mathematics but in particular my Latina students, who were often transnational students whose first language was not English. Finally, drawn from my role as a university professor working with future mathematics teachers, I offer recommendations for improving the retention of Latinas into mathematics as a

New Directions for Higher Education, no. 163, Fall 2013 © Wiley Periodicals, Inc.
Published online in Wiley Online Library (wileyonlinelibrary.com) • DOI:10.1002/he.20063

discipline. Using this perspective, my chapter presents an overview of the factors that most influence choices and success: families, schools, and higher education institutions.

Parents, Home, and Mathematics

Success in mathematics largely depends on home environment, parental support, and socioeconomic status. As a result, class issues may affect Latinas' academic performance. In many cases, although Latino parents value education, they can offer limited financial support for school; therefore, Latinas have to work to finance their own college education and/or pay for tuition and books through scholarships and financial aid. Socioeconomic status and financial aid sources subsequently impact their chances of completing a postsecondary degree. A great number of Latina students feel pressured to work and often must balance work and school to provide for themselves and many times also for their families (National Women's Law Center & Mexican American Legal Defense and Educational Fund, 2009; Seymour & Hewitt, 1997). However, socioeconomic status is not the only issue in terms of parental support. Cultural expectations also affect the kind of support students receive.

Like other ethnic groups, Latinos have explicit cultural values, such as honoring and valuing close familial relationships, respecting elders and authority, and maintaining the significance of faith and religion in the home (López-Baez, 1999). Latinos also define and adhere to clear-cut traditional gender roles. Although traditional gender roles are being challenged, many Latina students live in households where they are still practiced, so these students still hold responsibilities such as caretakers of younger siblings or older relatives. In addition, they are denied experiences that would positively affect their success in school; for example, significantly fewer Latina students than White students participate in sports or in extracurricular activities (Tomás Rivera Policy Institute, 2002). According to Villegas and Vincent (2005), Latina students receive more pressure from the family to honor cultural values and follow traditional ideals of gender roles (National Women's Law Center & Mexican American Legal Defense Educational Fund, 2009). Latinas are generally encouraged by their parents to be spiritual, nurturing, and self-sacrificing (López-Baez, 1999). In fact, some Latino parents may even discourage their daughters from pursuing higher education, especially in institutions that are far from home (Tomás Rivera Policy Institute, 2002).

Due to traditional values, Latinas often feel responsible for the family at a very young age; many are expected to do housework and take care of their elders and/or siblings. As a recent study found, these demands are forcing numerous Latina students to drop out of school and start working (Pew Hispanic Center, 2009). Some may even have to shoulder financial burdens and hold jobs to pay for their own school expenses. Low socioeconomic status negatively impacts students' achievement and success in school at all levels.

NEW DIRECTIONS FOR HIGHER EDUCATION • DOI:10.1002/he

When students do not have the needed resources, such as a place to study or access to reading materials or mathematical tools at home, grades suffer. Thus, the home environment, or the ecology of poor students' lives, affects their performance in schools.

Preparing for Higher Education

Given the fact that Latinas are the fastest growing group of female school-aged youth, high school teachers must recognize the critical connection between Latina students' motivation and their achievement in school, particularly in mathematics classes, as the teachers prepare them for higher education. Latinas should get an opportunity to develop high academic aspirations and to feel supported by their teachers in their desire to pursue higher-level education and more rigorous mathematics courses (Tomás Rivera Policy Institute, 2008). According to a nationwide study of the distribution of mathematics and science opportunities, students in high-minority schools had less than a 50% chance of being taught by mathematics or science teachers who held a degree or license in the field they taught (Darling-Hammond, 2010). Furthermore, these teachers experience the added pressure of preparing students, particularly Latinas, whom they may perceive as lacking mathematics proficiency. Latina students should nevertheless be encouraged to take key college preparatory courses such as algebra, known as the gatekeeper course to college success and disliked by many students in general. I believe that students' lack of identification with mathematics, especially algebra, lies in the disconnect many students feel with the methods and the content of algebra as it is currently taught. A culturally relevant pedagogy would address such disconnect.

Latinas deserve opportunities to study mathematics and science concepts that would prepare them for doctoral degrees in STEM fields. Additionally, they should be taught by adequately prepared teachers who believe in their Latina students' competence and who are trained in effective, culturally relevant methods of teaching. What is evident is the need for university teacher-preparation programs to satisfactorily prepare high school mathematics and science teachers. Teachers must hold special qualities and skills to meet the needs of Latina students, such as acknowledging the obstacles faced by them and genuinely caring about their success, as well as recognizing the skills that students may bring from home—their cultural capital, as it were. However, teachers must first believe that Latina students are capable learners, and they must understand that their cultural capital many times does not conform to traditional mainstream norms. In addition, they must see this unique cultural capital as an asset and not as a deficiency and use it as a teaching tool (Howard, 2003). Latinas must be prepared for the challenges of higher education. However, unfortunately, many poor school districts oftentimes do not adequately prepare minority students for college-level work in terms of curricula (Gándara & Contreras, 2009;

Tienda, 2009). Thus, a large number of underrepresented students lack proficiency and deep understanding of basic number sense, fractions, and measurement—basic concepts that are essential for mastering higher level and more demanding mathematics courses (Gándara & Contreras, 2009).

Students must receive an effective, rigorous, and relevant mathematical grounding as early as possible, but particularly in high school. Curricular issues such as fewer rigorous classes in their course of study result in poor preparation to tackle higher education and the rigors required in mathematics courses. According to the Tomás Rivera Policy Institute 2008 report, high schools with large minority populations tend to have less rigorous science and mathematics curricula. Additionally, in many instances underrepresented minorities disproportionately enroll in less demanding classes and have little access to more high-level classes, such as calculus, even when they are offered.

One of the most essential steps we can take to increase the likelihood of Latinas' academic success is motivating them to take the demanding classes that prepare them for college-level work. Schools should provide Latinas with rigorous higher-level mathematics classes that are engaging. Schools should also motivate Latinas to enroll and actively participate in mathematics courses, so that they will be ready and able to enter into the STEM fields with a good grasp of the mathematics required in college-level courses. I suggest that key elements in today's classrooms should include implementing a critical race curriculum that challenges racism and other forms of subordination present in traditional curriculum (Yosso, 2002) and utilizing a critical race pedagogy that "challenges White, middle-class, and male privilege in traditional pedagogical practices and creates spaces to learn from pedagogies of the home" (Yosso, Villalpando, Delgado Bernal, & Solórzano, 2001, p. 96).

Both critical race curriculum and pedagogy call for student engagement at an integrative level to manage the students' everyday lives as it enhances their education in relevant and significant ways. At times such integrative engagement may even touch on the students' emotions. A method that helps in increasing students' motivation to take responsibility for their learning is to get students emotionally involved in their own learning as they get ready to enter the higher education trajectory. Latinas face a number of obstacles in their educational trajectory (National Women's Law Center & Mexican American Legal Defense and Educational Fund, 2009; Portland State University Task Force on Latina/o Student Success, 2010; Tomás Rivera Policy Institute, 2008), and one of them is inadequate preparation for the demands of higher education (Cerna, Perez, & Sáenz, 2007).

Higher Education: Colleges, Universities, and Mathematics

By the time many Latina/o students have managed to survive elementary, middle, and high school and have been admitted to college, they often perceive it to be too late to get back on track in order to complete a higher education in the same time period as their non-Latino peers. Swail, Cabrera, and Lee (2004) have found that once in college, Latina students face a challenging future, one that requires more effort to stay on par with their non-Latino counterparts. They note that on their way to earn a college degree, Latina students face "an upward struggle" (p. 32) every step of the way and have challenges that are "enormous at best, impossible at worst" (p. vii). It is even more so for those seeking a graduate degree in the STEM disciplines.

The data on Latinas in higher education make it clear that not all of them have positive experiences. They oftentimes function within an education system that does not support them. Just as they did in prior schooling, they again encounter language barriers, poor curricula, low expectations, a lack of role models, and other such hurdles. Not all of the Latina students are instilled with the same sense of personal agency to enable them to overcome systemic problems in higher education, which often include racist and sexist microaggressions (such as being called "sweetie" or "mamacita"). Not all have someone encouraging them to succeed and daring them to try new things and test new ideas. It should be the role of their university professors to encourage their personal agency and drive and nurture their innate *ganas*, their inner motivation, to succeed.

In addition to being unprepared or having their ability questioned, many minority students rarely encounter faculty of color in their education who might serve as mentors and/or role models. When minority students connect with professors of the same ethnicity, they seem to be encouraged to pursue an academic career and become professors themselves. When a Latina student encounters a Latina professor, aside from sharing ethnicity, she is also able to reference the same cultural signifiers. The professor serves as a role model, yes, but more importantly, the student feels as if there is hope that she, too, can perform well and succeed.

Finally, students' success in obtaining a doctoral degree in STEM fields largely depends on their experiences in the home with their family and in the school and university with their teachers and professors. Based on my experiences and observations as a teacher of mathematics and as a professor preparing mathematics teachers for diverse classrooms, I believe the following recommendations are necessary to begin enabling Latinas to imagine themselves with a doctoral degree and to help instill in them the *ganas,* that inner desire to achieve and the confidence to embrace and succeed in STEM. In other words, the motivation to pursue careers in mathematics and in STEM fields is the key.

Recommendations for Motivating Latinas in Mathematics

Some of these recommendations overlap, and they are important for schools as well as for colleges and universities to heed. First and foremost a rigorous curriculum during the high school years and even earlier is critical; students need more demanding high school mathematics curricula and standards to help them become critical thinkers and leaders, to encourage them to have higher expectations of themselves, and to believe that they can succeed. Higher-level mathematics should be required of all students. Basic mathematics provides a foundation, but more advanced courses (beyond algebra) must be available for all high school students so that they will be ready to proceed onto a college or university campus.

Precollege programs should also be made available to students to make the transition to higher education easier. More funding and awareness of programs like Communities in Schools, Upward Bound, Tech-Prep Programs, dual enrollment, and early admission are needed. These programs help promote higher education and provide underrepresented minority students with hope (and training) for attaining a college degree. These programs must be staffed by individuals who are advocates for STEM education and who believe that minority and other underrepresented students possess the necessary skills to undertake rigorous college-level courses.

Numerous Latinas and other English language learners find language to be a barrier. To combat the limitation that limited English proficiency (LEP) constitutes for students, high schools, colleges, and universities must provide language development opportunities, but they must also value the primary language of the students. Students' own culture should be valued, and lessons should be relevant to their cultural background.

Teacher education programs should provide preservice teachers with training on how to integrate critical race and ethno-mathematics teaching techniques and practice in using engaging teaching strategies and pedagogy to help spark a love of learning in Latina students. We need to provide more culturally competent curricula in college and university classrooms that eliminate cultural barriers to understanding the language of mathematics and that ground mathematics in the real lives of students of diverse backgrounds. In addition, the digital divide must be addressed by bringing more technological learning resources into the classrooms of poor communities.

It is imperative for students to see and meet others like themselves succeeding in STEM fields, so they may in turn become aware of the possibility of their own success. Colleges and universities need to diversify their faculty, and if they are identified as Hispanic Serving Institutions, then their faculty should also reflect that demographic profile. More programs that make successful Latinas visible to their students should be implemented.

We need to provide minorities with awareness of financial aid opportunities so that they can obtain college and graduate degrees in a timely manner. Latina students, many of whom come from low- and middle-class families, might lack the financial means to fund a college career. Oftentimes, these families are not familiar with college admissions processes and availability of financial aid; they may have misguided perceptions of college costs, which may be forcing some students to forgo a college education.

Additionally, more opportunities should be provided for Latinas to advance their education within their own communities. The issue of access to quality and excellent education remains critical for the Latino community. This access will serve the dual purpose of creating successful role models who are visible within the community and increasing the number of Latinas who are successful in mathematics and in STEM careers.

Conclusion

It is crucial that we not ignore the benefits and advantages that educating Latinas in mathematics will bring, including their success in the STEM fields. One benefit of educating Latinas in mathematics and preparing them to enter STEM fields is that they will be ready to take over positions of an increasing number of professionals who are expected to retire in the near future (Tomás Rivera Policy Institute, 2008). Increasing the number of Latinas in STEM fields matters to them and their families because it opens doors and creates opportunities. But it matters most because "the safety of the nation and the quality of life—not just the prosperity of the nation—are at issue" (National Mathematics Advisory Panel, 2008, p. xi).

I have examined concerns that I deem critical as they affect the motivation of Latina students, and I have used my experience as a university professor to arrive at some observations and recommendations with the aim of attracting Latinas into the fields of science, technology, engineering, or mathematics. My discussion focused on the factors that most intimately affect choices and success for such students: the schools, colleges, and universities as well as the teachers and professors.

Throughout this chapter, my goal has been to bring to light the obstacles and struggles encountered by Latinas as they navigate through the school systems and on to the college/university classroom. My overarching goal has been not to focus only on the obstacles but on what I feel can be solutions so that Latina students "may be empowered" (Anzaldúa, 2002, p. 540) to meet and successfully move through higher education and come out with a doctoral degree. The challenge is for us to motivate and support Latinas in their educational trajectory at home, in the community, in schools, and in colleges and universities so that they can enter, persist, and receive a postsecondary education and a terminal degree, particularly in the STEM fields.

References

Anzaldúa, G. (2002). Now let us shift ... the path of conocimiento ... inner work, public acts. In G. Anzaldúa & A. Keating (Eds.), *This bridge we call home* (pp. 540–578). New York, NY: Routledge.

Cerna, O. S., Perez, P. A., & Sáenz, V. (2007). *Examining the pre-college attributes and values of Latina/o college graduates* (Higher Education Research Institute Research Report, No. 3). Retrieved from http://www.heri.ucla.edu/PDFs/pubs/Reports/LatinoRetention_Report3.pdf

Darling-Hammond, L. (2010). *The flat world and education: How America's commitment to equity will determine our future.* New York, NY: Teachers College Press.

Gándara, P., & Contreras, F. (2009). *The Latino education crisis: The consequences of failed social policies.* Cambridge, MA: Harvard University Press.

Howard, T. C. (2003). Culturally relevant pedagogy: Ingredients for critical teacher reflection. *Theory into Practice, 42*(3), 195–202.

Lopéz-Baez, S. (1999). Marianismo. In J. S. Mio, J. E. Trimble, P. Arredondo, H. E. Cheatham, & D. Sue (Eds.), *Key words in multicultural interventions: A dictionary* (p. 183). Westport, CT: Greenwood.

National Mathematics Advisory Panel. (2008). *Foundations for success: The final report of the National Mathematics Advisory Panel.* Washington, DC: U.S. Department of Education.

National Women's Law Center (NWLC) & Mexican American Legal Defense and Educational Fund (MALDEF). (2009). *Listening to Latinas: Barriers to high school graduation.* Washington, DC: Author.

Pew Hispanic Center. (2009). *Between two worlds: How young Latinos come of age in America.* Washington, DC: Author.

Portland State University Task Force on Latina/o Student Success. (2010). *Exito! A path to Latino student success.* Retrieved from www.pdx.edu/sites/www.pdx.edu.diversity/files/exito_report.pdf

Seymour, E., & Hewitt, N. M. (1997). *Talk about leaving: Why undergraduates leave the sciences.* Boulder, CO: Westview Press.

Swail, W. S., Cabrera, A. F., & Lee, C. (2004). *Latino youth and the pathway to college.* Washington, DC: Educational Policy Institute.

Tienda, M. (2009, March). *Hispanicity and educational inequality: Risks, opportunities and the nation's future.* Tomás Rivera Lecture Series. Paper presented at the annual conference of the American Association of Hispanics in Higher Education (AAHHE), San Antonio, TX.

Tomás Rivera Policy Institute. (2002). *Latinos and information technology: The promise and the challenge.* Los Angeles, CA: Author.

Tomás Rivera Policy Institute. (2008). *STEM professions: Opportunities and challenges for Latinos in science, technology, engineering, and mathematics: A review of literature.* Los Angeles, CA: Author.

Villegas, M. A. S., & Vincent, K. M. (2005). Factors that influence the underrepresentation of Latino/a students majoring in mathematics in the state of Washington. *WSU McNair Journal, 3,* 114–129.

Yosso, T. (2002). Toward a critical race curriculum. *Journal of Equity and Excellence in Education, 35*(2), 93–107. doi:10.1080/713845283

Yosso, T., Villalpando, O., Delgado Bernal, D., & Solórzano, D. G. (2001, April). *Critical race theory in Chicana/o education.* Paper presented at the National Association for Chicana and Chicano Studies Annual Conference, Tucson, AZ. Retrieved from http://scholarworks.sjsu.edu/naccs/2001/Proceedings/9

ELSA C. RUIZ is assistant professor of curriculum and instruction at The University of Texas at San Antonio.

4

Students who are the first in their families to graduate from college have significant challenges and yet comprise a significant percentage of the number of awarded doctorates in the United States.

The Challenges of First-Generation Doctoral Students

Susan K. Gardner

In 2010, nearly one-third (32.1%) of all doctoral recipients reported being first-generation students (National Science Foundation & National Center for Science and Engineering Statistics, 2012), meaning that their parents did not complete an undergraduate degree (Choy, 2001; Nunez & Cuccaro-Alamin, 1998; Pascarella, Pierson, Wolniak, & Terenzini, 2004). First-generation doctoral students tend to have unique characteristics that set them apart from their non-first-generation peers and create distinctive challenges. First-generation doctoral students also tend to come from particular demographic groups and are concentrated in certain academic disciplines. For example, these students are more likely to be students of color and to be more highly concentrated in applied academic fields such as education and engineering (National Science Foundation & National Center for Science and Engineering Statistics, 2012). Therefore, it is important to examine the intersectionality of the different identities that first-generation doctoral students bring to their experiences.

The purpose of this chapter is to discuss the issues and challenges faced by first-generation doctoral students, with a particular focus on doctoral students of color. Students of color remain underrepresented in doctoral education. When coupled with a first-generation status, such students may face particular issues and challenges that could ultimately impede their retention and success.

First-Generation Students

Although there are many definitions of first-generation status, for the purposes of this chapter first-generation students are defined as being from

NEW DIRECTIONS FOR HIGHER EDUCATION, no. 163, Fall 2013 © Wiley Periodicals, Inc.
Published online in Wiley Online Library (wileyonlinelibrary.com) • DOI:10.1002/he.20064

families where neither parent has completed a college degree or beyond (Pascarella et al., 2004). At the undergraduate level, first-generation students are more likely than their non-first-generation peers to (a) be considered low-income, (b) be older, (c) be female, (d) have a disability, (e) come from minority backgrounds, (f) have dependent children, and (g) be financially independent from their parents. First-generation students are also less likely than their non-first-generation peers to aspire to, enroll in, and complete graduate education (Engle & Tinto, 2008).

Nevertheless, the proportion of first-generation students who persist to and complete a doctoral degree is significant, with 32.1% of all doctoral recipients in 2010 being first-generation. As shown in Table 4.1, when considered by race, individuals from non-White groups are more likely to be from first-generation families (National Science Foundation & National Center for Science and Engineering Statistics, 2012).

As presented in Table 4.2, first-generation doctoral students are also more likely to be concentrated in particular disciplines and professional fields, such as education, and to be least represented among the humanities (National Science Foundation & National Center for Science and Engineering Statistics, 2012).

Table 4.1. First-Generation 2010 Doctoral Recipients by Race

Racial Group	Percentage of First-Generation Doctoral Recipients
Asians	37.9%
Blacks	41.4%
Latinos	36.2%
Native Americans	57.2%
Whites	19.4%

Table 4.2. First-Generation Doctoral Recipients by Field of Study

Field of Study	Percentage of First-Generation Doctoral Students
Life Sciences	21.4%
Physical Sciences	21.6%
Social Sciences	20.8%
Engineering	21.0%
Education	29.2%
Humanities	18.9%

However, these statistics are all self-reported from those who complete the doctoral degree and do not offer insight into the likelihood of particular groups completing the degree in the first place. When considering other statistics about doctoral completion by different demographic groups, the unique characteristics of the first-generation students become more salient. For example, while 57% of all doctoral candidates will graduate within 10 years (Council of Graduate Schools, 2008a), when broken down by disciplinary group and by racial group, these numbers vary widely. For example, as presented in Table 4.3, 64% of those with a degree in engineering will graduate as compared to only 49% of those in the humanities. Cumulatively, those with degrees in STEM fields (science, technology, engineering, and mathematics) are more likely to complete the doctoral degree than those in non-STEM fields, such as the humanities (Council of Graduate Schools, 2008a).

Comparing the doctoral completion rates of racial groups, disparities become even clearer. "While completion rates for all students may be lower than optimal, the 'failure to complete' problem is notably more serious among students from underrepresented populations: both women and minorities," concluded the Council of Graduate Schools (2008b, p. 1). Such disparities are even more salient among students of color in STEM disciplines, where there has been significant national attention to increasing the retention and success of these groups (National Science Foundation, 2004a, 2004b). Table 4.4 presents enrollment by race in particular disciplines as reported by the Council of Graduate Schools (2008b), demonstrating a high representation of students of color in the social sciences and an underrepresentation of students of color in the STEM fields.

At the same time, the completion rates for these doctoral student groups do not remain consistent with their enrollment trends. For example, while the majority of students of color will be found in the social sciences, only 47% of African Americans, 46% of Asian Americans, and 37% of Latinos who begin the degree will actually complete it. Table 4.5 presents completion rates by racial group in academic fields (Council of Graduate Schools, 2008b).

Taken together, while doctoral education has seen a substantial increase in students of color in the past decades, they still remain underrepresented in degree programs and demonstrate lower completion rates

Table 4.3. PhD Completion Rates by Field of Study

Field of Study	10-Year Completion Rate
Engineering	64%
Life Sciences	63%
Social Sciences	56%
Mathematics and Physical Sciences	55%
Humanities	49%

Table 4.4. Distribution of Doctoral Students by Field of Study

Racial Group	Engineering	Life Sciences	Mathematics & Physical Sciences	Humanities	Social Sciences
African American	8%	14%	10%	13%	55%
Asian/Pacific Islander	20%	23%	18%	11%	27%
Latino American	6%	21%	16%	19%	38%
Native Americans, Alaska Natives, Multiracial	13%	19%	12%	23%	33%
Whites	9%	19%	16%	19%	37%

Table 4.5. Cumulative 10-year PhD Completion Rates by Race/Ethnicity and Academic Field

Racial Group	Engineering	Life Sciences	Mathematics & Physical Sciences	Humanities	Social Sciences
African American	47%	60%	37%	52%	47%
Asian American	53%	47%	53%	44%	46%
Latino American	55%	54%	53%	55%	37%
Whites	60%	60%	52%	57%	51%

compared to their peers. While the Council of Graduate Schools did not seek to examine first-generation status within its 1992–2004 study, it is known that students of color tend to be overrepresented among first-generation doctoral students (Hoffer et al., 2002).

Challenges of First-Generation Doctoral Students

While it could certainly be said that graduate school is challenging for all students (Nettles & Millett, 2006), extant literature has noted specific challenges endemic to the first-generation student population. Below I highlight several of these challenges, drawing on the literature as well as my own research data.

Understanding the System of Graduate Education. In a 2002 special report of the Survey of Earned Doctorates (Hoffer et al., 2002), some of the issues and challenges facing first-generation doctoral students were outlined. Hoffer and colleagues concluded, "These students are likely to have faced special challenges in the course of earning the doctorate, for their parents are likely to have lower incomes and perhaps less knowledge to share about how to negotiate college and graduate school" (p. 34). In other words, simply getting to graduate school is only half of the battle for these students. While many first-generation undergraduate students will struggle to understand financial aid processes and other taken-for-granted processes and procedures in higher education (Pascarella et al., 2004; Terenzini, Springer, Yaeger, Pascarella, & Nora, 1996), undergraduate colleges and universities have begun providing more targeted assistance for these students in recent decades. Moreover, representations of college life are prevalent in popular culture, providing a rudimentary (if not wholly accurate) roadmap for first-generation students.

Graduate students, however, still tend to be a largely "traditional" population in that the majority of them come from families where not only do their parents have undergraduate degrees, but also large numbers hold advanced degrees (National Science Foundation, 2010). In other words, the majority of doctoral students are second generation or beyond, using their family's collected history and knowledge to inform their graduate school experiences. First-generation doctoral students, on the other hand, tend to have undergraduate degrees from schools without doctoral programs and are more likely to have attended community college for part of their undergraduate experience (Hoffer et al., 2002). Without models from home, from popular culture, or from their undergraduate education, many of these first-generation doctoral students struggle to understand the "rules" of graduate education, or what Lovitts (2001) referred to as the "cognitive map" of graduate school.

Cognitive maps are "mental models that are created jointly by members of a community and give coherence to perceptions of events, people, and objects" (Lovitts, 2001, p. 44). These cognitive maps assist individuals in making sense of their experiences and allow them to better understand their environments in order to make more informed decisions about their lives and future plans (Lovitts, 2001). Cognitive maps can be gained from interactions with advisors, more advanced graduate students, and even program materials such as student handbooks. Without accurate cognitive maps for each of the different stages of the graduate school experience (entry, coursework, examination, and dissertation), students may struggle to persist in the graduate program. For example, in our study of first-generation doctoral students (Gardner & Holley, 2011; Holley & Gardner, 2012), Karri Holley and I found that first-generation students often do not even know the questions they should ask, much less to whom they should be asked. This disconnect requires a high level of independence and self-direction on the part of these students. One student recounted, "I see in certain things that being first-generation makes it harder. I had to study twice as hard to learn how to maneuver in and out of the system, how to work the system, and how to learn. I had to learn this. No one taught me anything. I am learning it as I go" (Gardner & Holley, 2011, p. 84). Another student summarized, "Everything rests on you. There is no other reference point."

Financial Constraints. Another issue for many first-generation students relates to financial support and understanding how to manage financial demands. Research has shown that first-generation doctoral students tend to have higher debt loads than their non-first-generation peers (Hoffer et al., 2002). In their 2002 report, Hoffer and colleagues stated that first-generation doctoral recipients were more likely to identify their own resources as their primary source of support, as opposed to non-first-generation students, who were more likely to hold graduate teaching or research assistantships or grants and fellowships to finance their graduate education. Moreover, African Americans and Latino Americans were more likely than Asians and Whites to have high levels of education-related debt upon graduation (Hoffer et al., 2002). In our study (Gardner & Holley, 2011; Holley & Gardner, 2012), we heard first-generation students repeatedly voicing their concerns about the debt they were incurring. One student who held a graduate assistantship explained,

> For me to survive—and that is really what it is about: survival—I have to have a second job. The only way I am able to survive is on student loans. When I get out of this I am going to have a ton of debt. (Gardner & Holley, 2011, p. 86)

She further reflected on the hefty financial burden:

> I've tried to think about it as an investment and not let it bother me, but there are times when it is really overwhelming. I am essentially going to have a loan that is the price of what I could purchase a house for.

Financial Support and Time to Degree. Financial support and time to degree are negatively correlated in doctoral education (Abedi & Benkin, 1987; Bowen & Rudenstine, 1992; DesJardins, Ahlburg, & McCall, 2002), meaning that the more financial support students have, the less time it takes for them to complete their degrees. Given the tendency of first-generation doctoral students to have less financial support than their non-first-generation peers, it is not surprising that these students are also more likely to register higher time-to-degree rates than their non-first-generation peers (Hoffer et al., 2002). These higher rates of time to degree may owe to both financial reasons as well as the issues that Lovitts (2001) discussed in relation to cognitive mapping. For example, some first-generation doctoral students may not understand that fellowships or assistantships exist to support their graduate education, instead believing they must pay for their graduate education as they did for their undergraduate—through loans or grants. Given the fact that little federal financial aid is available to graduate students other than loans, first-generation students may feel stymied by the lack of options. One student expressed, "I didn't know that there was such a thing as a graduate assistantship until I was offered one." As a result, many first-generation students, like those in our study, may feel like they have to seek outside employment to afford graduate school, thereby delaying their progress.

First-generation students are also more likely than their non-first-generation peers to be older and have dependents (Terenzini et al., 1996). The first-generation doctoral students in our study often discussed the metaphorical tug of war they played in balancing their graduate school responsibilities with their families at home. One woman explained her situation: "The kids' dad is a deadbeat and doesn't pay much child support, and what time I can put into a job is not enough to cover it." She shared her employment experiences:

> I've taught classes, I've worked full-time jobs, and I take a full load and always have, and I get what I need from the loans. I've tried to limit myself as much as I can on the loans, but I can't shortchange the time I have to spend with my kids. (Holley & Gardner, 2012, p. 118)

Even those first-generation doctoral students in our study who did not have dependents expressed the need to remain close to home to assist with their families' needs, especially those of aging parents. Indeed, first-generation students are more likely than their non-first-generation peers to choose an educational institution based upon its proximity to their home; for example, one study found that these students stayed within 50 miles of their homes when choosing institutions of higher education (Higher Education Research Institute, 2007). These sentiments were repeated by first-generation students in our study. One woman told us, "I decided to come back to be close to home because my parents are getting older, their health is starting to fail." Some students made the choice to remain at the institution where they completed their undergraduate degree as it felt more comfortable. Another woman discussed her experience: "I went to visit other schools, and I understood that they were more prestigious, but I wasn't ready. I don't think I even understood what a graduate degree meant. I think that's why I stayed here for the PhD." She concluded, "I was in a place where I felt supported, comforted, and valued." Another said her options were limited because of her children. When asked why she chose her institution, she remarked, "There's not much choice in the state. I couldn't go elsewhere. I have a family and I can't just pack up and leave. So, convenience, I guess."

Feelings of Otherness. The financial concerns discussed by the students were often more than simply dollars and cents to them; they were also emblematic of the feeling of "otherness" that many of them felt as a result of being first-generation. In our study, we referred to this experience as belonging in "two worlds" (Gardner & Holley, 2011, p. 84), wherein the first-generation students sought to belong to the academic world while reconciling the poverty that many had come from. One student explained, "It was incredibly difficult at first. I felt completely lost. It was clear that I was the only student in the department whose parents didn't go to college." He concluded, "All the people I met had parents who were headmasters at private schools and all sorts of things. My mom works at Wal-Mart and my dad is an electrician. I just felt strange because I didn't have a reference" (Holley & Gardner, 2012, p. 118). He reflected on the impact of this perspective: "I didn't have anybody to tell me how to get through this. It was also difficult to explain to my parents what I was doing or why I was doing it" (p. 118). Another student described the experience, saying,

> I sit in class and listen to the other students and think that these people know this stuff because they get it from their parents and I'm like the pioneer out there with my little wagon, not always knowing what I'm doing. But I'm doing it anyway.

An African American woman explained,

> I really don't belong here in terms of class, in terms of gender, in terms of race. I don't belong. And everything is saying that I don't belong, but I am getting messages that say I do belong and I do have a place here. (Gardner & Holley, 2011, p. 85)

Many of the students also talked about having difficulties feeling they belonged in either world. For example, students discussed how difficult it was to go back home after being exposed to the education that their family and friends lacked. One student said,

> It's hard going home because people think that you think you're better than them. You're a black sheep in a different kind of way. No one wants to talk about school because they don't understand it, but because it's such a big part of your life you don't have anything else to talk about. It can be very uncomfortable. One thing I've had to learn is to watch the vocabulary I use.

She provided this example: "I have to be very careful because I'll say something when I'm home and they'll say, 'What does that mean?' and I tell them and then they say, 'Why didn't you just say that? Why does it take four words instead of two?' It doesn't go well."

For the students of color in our study, these feelings of otherness were even more salient. One African American woman stated,

> This is a predominately White school so you can feel isolated here. You can be in a crowd of people who look like you but you're not feeling that you belong here. The students who come from families who had gone through college come here with a leg up. They are able to focus readily and they have the support and help with writing. They have parents and friends they can show their work to.

Another African American man sighed and explained,

I have literally cut off all connections to those people back home because those people are doing things that I cannot be associated with. It hurts. I'm still living in this dream that doesn't call for reality: the reality of me remembering where I come from. (Holley & Gardner, 2012, p. 118)

Imposter Phenomenon. This sense of otherness expressed by students in our study was also closely related to what can be termed *imposter syndrome* or the *imposter phenomenon*. First considered with women in high-achieving positions who did not feel as if they belonged (Clance, 1985; Clance & Imes, 1978; Clance & O'Toole, 1987), studies of the imposter phenomenon have also been conducted with students of color at the graduate level (i.e., Ewing, Richardson, James-Myers, & Russell, 1996). The imposter phenomenon can be defined as "an internal experience of intellectual phoniness" (Clance & Imes, 1978, p. 241). In Clance and Imes's work, the imposter phenomenon was often discovered among women who believed they were not intelligent and that luck or mistakes accounted for their success. As a result, they lived in constant fear of being discovered as a fraud.

In our study (Gardner & Holley, 2011; Holley & Gardner, 2012), the imposter phenomenon was prevalent particularly among women and students of color. One woman whispered, "The hardest thing is thinking that someone is going to find out that I really shouldn't be here, even though it is something that I have fought so hard for." She started to cry at this point, murmuring, "I have to remind myself constantly that I have a right to be here. I have to keep telling myself that" (Gardner & Holley, 2011, p. 85).

Implications and Recommendations

First-generation doctoral students face myriad challenges in their graduate programs. While some of these challenges are endemic to the graduate experience, others are particular to their backgrounds. I offer here recommendations for those working with these students to further support and facilitate their persistence based on the challenges presented earlier.

Academic Guidance and Mentoring. First-generation doctoral students tend to be drawn to applied disciplines, such as those in the social sciences and in education (National Science Foundation, 2010). Much research has been conducted on why underrepresented populations, such as women in STEM and students of color, are attracted to particular fields of study over others. Often, the rationale for the choice of field is based upon the desire to "make a difference in the world," which is reflected in the degree choice of many first-generation students. Faculty and academic advisors can assist in recruiting these students to their fields by discussing the real-world implications of their work. Similarly, many of these students are drawn to the field of education. In my study with Karri Holley, we found that many of the first-generation participants were first interested in pursuing a PhD because of a desire to emulate their mentors, such as an influential professor. Providing first-generation students with teaching opportunities and research-related professional development opportunities may serve as an incentive for these students' retention.

Regardless of field, it is also clear that first-generation students tend to have a longer time to degree than their non-first-generation peers. Given their lack of a cognitive map (Lovitts, 2001), first-generation students can greatly benefit from explicit mentoring and guidance in their graduate programs. Orientation sessions, mentoring programs that pair new students with more advanced students, and detailed program handbooks will all be helpful to these students.

Financial Support. Not all first-generation students are aware of the financial resources that exist to support their education. First-generation students may benefit from messages as early as high school and undergraduate education that inform them how graduate education operates and can be funded. Particularly at institutions that do not have doctoral programs—where many first-generation students are drawn (Hoffer et al., 2002)—providing these messages to students is important. Undergraduate programs may also consider implementing visitation programs to local graduate schools for those who are considering graduate education, similar to activities enacted by efforts like the McNair Scholars Program.

At the same time, many first-generation students may feel the need to remain close to home and not always understand the full array of options available to them and how these choices may later impact career decisions (such as how the choice of a doctoral program influences future career opportunities in academia). Again, early advising in the undergraduate years can assist these students in understanding the pipeline as well as how these more "implicit" messages of academia operate.

Universities should also consider implementing funding specific to first-generation students. While not all first-generation students will be aware of assistantship or fellowship funding, most are well aware of how the FAFSA operates and the concepts of loans and scholarships after completing their undergraduate degrees. Providing new graduate students with an online orientation to the array of financial options may also be helpful in this regard. Programs and graduate schools might also consider providing an online checklist of the possible funding options that is directly connected to the application.

Fostering Feelings of Belonging. Discussed quite often by the students in our study was the feeling that many of them had about otherness or not belonging. While the representation of first-generation doctoral students will vary by discipline as well as by institution (i.e., they tend to be more represented in less prestigious institutions), many students may simply not be aware of others who share their experience. A feeling of belonging may be engendered through creating a welcoming atmosphere for all students. For example, in graduate classes that I teach, I always make it a point in the first meeting to discuss my own first-generation status. I have seen repeatedly how this self-disclosure has invited other first-generation students to approach me with their experiences and concerns. Similarly, providing connections among students who might be first-generation through a peer mentoring program or even a student organization sponsored through the graduate school might be helpful to this population.

Related, often these students may not feel they belong simply as a result of feeling they are not so connected or knowledgeable as their peers. If all students are provided with the access to the same resources and information, then there is no "insider" information to be gained by some people and not others. Namely, making the implicit explicit, as Lovitts (2007) suggested, in all phases and parts of the doctoral program will be helpful not only to first-generation students, but also to all students. Obviously, what is implicit to one individual may be explicit to another; in other words, what faculty may find clear students may deem unclear. Faculty and graduate coordinators could coordinate with more advanced students to provide a listing of resources and information advanced students wish they had known upon entering.

Finally, it is important to note the special support that first-generation doctoral students of color may require. Work by scholars such as Barker (2010) has pointed to the need to create supportive environments for doctoral students of color, particularly in predominantly White institutions. These students may face increased feelings of isolation and "otherness" as a result of their underrepresented status. Providing university-wide student organizations, peer mentoring programs, and connections to scholars of color outside of the university may facilitate their retention and success.

In sum, the first-generation doctoral student population is one that is highly represented on many campuses and in many disciplines but continues to face myriad challenges. Graduate schools, departments, and faculty can work together to create support for these students, thereby providing a path to success and graduation.

References

Abedi, J., & Benkin, E. (1987). The effects of students' academic, financial, and demographic variables on time to the doctorate. *Research in Higher Education, 27*(1), 3–14.

Barker, M. J. (2010). *Cross-race advising relationships: The role of race in advising relationships between Black doctoral student proteges and their White faculty advisors* (Unpublished doctoral dissertation). Louisiana State University, Baton Rouge.

Bowen, W. G., & Rudenstine, N. L. (1992). *In pursuit of the PhD.* Princeton, NJ: Princeton University Press.

Choy, S. P. (2001). *Students whose parents did not go to college: Postsecondary access, persistence, and attainment.* Jessup, MD: ED Pubs.

Clance, P. R. (1985). *The impostor phenomenon: Overcoming the fear that haunts your success.* Atlanta, GA: Peachtree Publishers.

Clance, P. R., & Imes, S. A. (1978). The impostor phenomenon in high achieving women: Dynamics and therapeutic intervention. *Psychotherapy: Theory, Research, and Practice, 15*, 241–247.

Clance, P. R., & O'Toole, M. A. (1987). The imposter phenomenon: An internal barrier to empowerment and achievement. *Women and Therapy, 6*(3), 51–64.

Council of Graduate Schools. (2008a). *Ph.D. completion and attrition: Analysis of baseline program data from the Ph.D. completion project.* Washington, DC: Author.
Council of Graduate Schools. (2008b). *Ph.D. completion and attrition: Analysis of baseline demographic data from the Ph.D. completion project.* Washington, DC: Author.
DesJardins, S. L., Ahlburg, D. A., & McCall, B. P. (2002). A temporal investigation of factors related to timely degree completion. *Journal of Higher Education, 73*(5), 555–581.
Engle, J., & Tinto, V. (2008). *Moving beyond access: College success for low-income, first-generation students.* Washington, DC: Pell Institute.
Ewing, K. M., Richardson, T. Q., James-Myers, L., & Russell, R. K. (1996). The relationship between racial identity attitudes, worldview, and African American graduate students' experience of the imposter phenomenon. *Journal of Black Psychology, 22,* 53–66.
Gardner, S. K., & Holley, K. A. (2011). "Those invisible barriers are real": The experiences of first-generation doctoral students. *Equity and Excellence in Education, 44,* 77–92.
Higher Education Research Institute. (2007). *First in my family.* Los Angeles: University of California, Los Angeles.
Hoffer, T. B., Welch, V., Webber, K., Williams, K., Lisek, B., Hess, M., ... Guzman-Barron, I. (2002). *Doctorate recipients from United States universities: Summary report 2002* (Vol. 2004). Chicago, IL: National Opinion Research Center.
Holley, K. A., & Gardner, S. K. (2012). Navigating the pipeline: How socio-cultural influences impact first-generation doctoral students. *Journal of Diversity in Higher Education, 5,* 112–121.
Lovitts, B. E. (2001). *Leaving the ivory tower: The causes and consequences of departure from doctoral study.* Lanham, MD: Rowman and Littlefield.
Lovitts, B. E. (2007). *Making the implicit explicit: Creating performance expectations for the dissertation.* Sterling, VA: Stylus.
National Science Foundation. (2004a). *Broadening participation in America's science and engineering workforce.* Washington, DC: Author.
National Science Foundation. (2004b). *Science and engineering degrees, by race/ethnicity of recipients: 1992-2001.* Arlington, VA: NSF Division of Science Resources Statistics.
National Science Foundation. (2010). *Doctorate recipients from U.S. universities: 2009* (Special Report NSF 11-306). Arlington, VA: Author.
National Science Foundation & National Center for Science and Engineering Statistics. (2012). *Doctorate recipients from U.S. universities: 2010.* Arlington, VA: Author.
Nettles, M. T., & Millett, C. M. (2006). *Three magic letters: Getting to Ph.D.* Baltimore, MD: The Johns Hopkins University Press.
Nunez, A. M., & Cuccaro-Alamin, S. (1998). *First-generation students: Undergraduates whose parents never enrolled in postsecondary education.* Washington, DC: National Center for Education Statistics.
Pascarella, E. T., Pierson, C. T., Wolniak, G. C., & Terenzini, P. T. (2004). First-generation college students: Additional evidence on college experiences and outcomes. *Journal of Higher Education, 75*(3), 249–284.
Terenzini, P. T., Springer, L., Yaeger, P. M., Pascarella, E. T., & Nora, A. (1996). First-generation college students: Characteristics, experiences, and cognitive development. *Research in Higher Education, 37*(1), 1–22.

SUSAN K. GARDNER is associate professor of higher education at the University of Maine, where she also serves as the director of the National Science Foundation ADVANCE Rising Tide Center.

NEW DIRECTIONS FOR HIGHER EDUCATION • DOI:10.1002/he

5

Doctoral students can face unique obstacles in terms of balancing the demands of a graduate program with personal obligations.

Family-Friendly Policies for Doctoral Students

Jaime Lester

Todd, a doctoral student with a teaching assistant job, expresses to his peers and faculty mentors that he may need to take a leave from graduate school to undergo an invasive surgery. The recovery time is two months. He is told that graduate students are ineligible for family and medical leave and he will need to resign from his assistantship for the semester.

Mary, a doctoral student in the sciences, is directly and explicitly told by her female faculty mentor not to pursue a faculty job, because balancing faculty research expectations conflicts with Mary's desire to have a family. She should consider work in a research institute or federal laboratory where she can have a "typical" job and not be concerned with getting tenure.

Sabrina's father has just called with devastating news regarding her mother's health. Sabrina will need to leave graduate school for a few weeks. Her faculty advisor is very supportive and suggests that Sabrina take the time she needs. But when weeks start to turn into months, Sabrina is forced to resign her assistantship and it is given to another graduate student. Sabrina has no guarantees that her assistantship will start again when she is able to return to graduate school.

Rose just gave birth to her first child and timed the delivery so that the child was born in the summer months and would not conflict with her research assistant position in a competitive humanities doctoral program. She returned to work in the fall without a private office and little to no access to a locked and private room. She now has to pump breast milk in her car, as the university has not established a lactation room on campus.

Over the last few decades, considerable attention has been paid to work–life balance for faculty. From parenting on the tenure track to phased retirement, individual institutions, philanthropic organizations, national

New Directions for Higher Education, no. 163, Fall 2013 © Wiley Periodicals, Inc.
Published online in Wiley Online Library (wileyonlinelibrary.com) • DOI:10.1002/he.20065

associations, and academic research have shed light on the complexity of work–life issues for tenured or tenure-line faculty. The term *work–life balance* is generally understood as the ability of an individual to balance work and home responsibilities to achieve a meaningful life. In organizations, work–life balance translates into programs and policies to support workplace and career flexibility. These efforts are reflected in a series of programs in academe that include tenure clock adjustment; flexible work arrangements, such as modified work schedules with a reduction in duties; paid and extended leave policies for childbirth, adoption, eldercare, or disability leave; and phased retirement (Lester & Sallee, 2009). Work–life issues influence female academics at a higher rate than men. Female faculty with children leave academe at a disproportionately higher rate than men. Such women cite pressure to postpone pregnancy or forgo childbearing to acquire tenure. Others refuse to make use of existing work–life policies, such as stopping the tenure clock, for fear of expectations from colleagues regarding productivity (Armenti, 2004; Drago et al., 2005; Finkel, Olswang, & She, 1994; Mason & Goulden, 2002; Monroe, Ozyurta, Wrigleya, & Alexander, 2008; Sullivan, Hollenshead, & Smith, 2004; Ward & Wolf-Wendel, 2004; Yoest, 2004). A more recent study noted the role of institutional context, specifically supportive departments, as influencing faculty members' "feeling that the individual has the power to make decisions that are the best for his or her balance of personal and professional lives" (O'Meara & Campbell, 2011, p. 448). Only recently has research on male faculty uncovered that institutional structures and cultures, such as expectations for teaching and committee meetings outside normal business hours and taking time off after birth of a child, penalize men who appear too committed to their families (Sallee, 2011).

Other constituent populations on college campuses, including staff, contingent faculty, and graduate students, have received far less attention compared to tenured or tenure-line faculty. As noted in the four short vignettes, graduate students exhibit a host of unique issues around work–life that begin from one significant distinction: Graduate students who hold teaching or research assistantships directly related to their educational program are generally not considered employees and, therefore, do not have access to the federal Family and Medical Leave Act. These graduate students do not have rights that extend beyond the undergraduate student population, despite the fact that they often receive institutional funding for teaching or research assistant positions. Graduate students may need to take a leave for pregnancy, adoption, or an illness of their own or of a family member; yet, as expressed through the vignettes of Todd and Sabrina, paid assistantships may not continue or be available upon return from a family or medical event. Simply put, graduate students have no job protection or access to paid or unpaid leave. In a recent analysis of organizational culture on several college campuses identified as having progressive work–life policies, I found progressive policies with paid leave for tenured or tenure-earning faculty *only* and little to no protections (or paid leave) for all other constituent groups on campus, including graduate students (Lester, 2013). What I found was a culture of inequity that privileged faculty over and above all other employment contracts.

The purpose of this chapter is to shed light on the complexity of work–life issues for doctoral students. National data indicate that only 41% of doctoral students complete their degrees in seven years and 57% in ten years (Council of Graduate Schools, 2008). While research has not made the causal connection between doctoral attrition and work–life issues, the experiences and struggle of doctoral students who work and learn at a university for two to ten (or more) years are important to understand and consider in institutional policy development. Moreover, the demographics of graduate students are changing with an increasing number of women, students of color, and international students (U.S. Department of Education, 2003). These groups arguably have different work–life needs that may require a new look at policies and practices within universities. For example, an international student may need to take several weeks off from graduate school to travel home for a family medical event or may require housing over the summer months due to the distance from campus to his or her family.

Following is a review of the literature on work–life issues related to graduate students. I argue that institutions of higher education need to consider reframing the employment status of graduate students to include work–life benefits traditionally only available to tenured and tenure-earning faculty. By having these benefits, graduate students are less likely to experience disruptions in their degree progress and more likely to complete their educational goals. Furthermore, local department cultures need to develop values related to work–life balance to support graduate student retention. This chapter concludes with a series of specific recommendations with examples from higher education institutions to support work–life balance for doctoral students. My intention is to provide concrete advice and evidence of ways to support graduate students who serve higher education institutions as teaching and research assistants and play an integral role in supporting the institution's core functions.

Throughout this chapter, I use graduate students and doctoral students interchangeably. However, the content of this chapter refers to full-time graduate students who often have paid part-time graduate student assistantships on campuses. This definition does not preclude the recommendations from applying to part-time graduate students, who often have more work–family conflicts (Brus, 2006).

Review of Literature on Graduate Students and Work–Life Balance

The literature on graduate students and work–life balance is relatively thin in comparison to the attention on tenure and tenure-earning faculty. Much

NEW DIRECTIONS FOR HIGHER EDUCATION • DOI:10.1002/he

of the research that does exist on graduate students identifies a concern on the part of these students in achieving work–life balance while in graduate school and in a future faculty role. Department and disciplinary cultures, as well as individual life circumstances that include multiple roles associated with family responsibilities, mediate these concerns. Research also indirectly connects work–life issues to retention in graduate school, as well as to reduced aspirations to entering the professoriate. Attention to the work–life needs of graduate students has the potential to support persistence and pathways to future faculty careers.

A significant consideration when discussing work–life balance and graduate education is changing demographics. Since the late 1980s, women have outpaced men in graduate enrollment (U.S. Department of Education, 2003). Women comprise 60% of all graduate students (U.S. Department of Education, 2011). Looking at the numbers of full-time versus part-time students shows similar trends. Between 2000 and 2010, the number of full-time male postbaccalaureate students increased by 38%, compared with a 62% increase in the number of full-time female postbaccalaureate students (U.S. Department of Education, 2011). Among part-time postbaccalaureate students, the number of males increased by 17% and the number of females increased by 26%. Increases in minority graduate enrollment also doubled to 20% by 2001, with similar increases for international students (U.S. Department of Education, 2003). These demographics are particularly significant given that women and people of color are more likely to have increased family responsibility, strongly associated with diminished academic success (Kerber, 2005; Mason & Goulden, 2002; Wagner, 2002). Moreover, periodic disruptions often caused by increased responsibilities predominately disadvantage women (Curtis, 2004; Williams, 2003; Younes & Asay, 1998). Colleges and universities are experiencing a demographic change in the graduate student population that requires additional considerations for work–life balance in order to continue to promote graduate student success.

Studies on work–life issues among graduate students confirm a need to consider the role of balance, a desire to have children, and a student's marriage or partnership status. One of the largest and most important studies of graduate students is that of Mason, Goulden, and Frasch (2009) who surveyed more than 8,000 doctoral students in the University of California system. They found that doctoral students were least satisfied with career–life balance and time for recreation and health. Over 60% of those surveyed desired to have children but felt uncertain about having children in graduate school. Mason and colleagues noted the following concerns of the doctoral students:

> Those planning to have children in the future cite many factors contributing to uncertainty about having children as doctoral students, including the time demands of PhD programs; current household income level; the perceived

stress of raising a child while a student; and concerns about the availability of affordable child care, housing, and health insurance. (p. 15)

Another mediating factor in the research on work–life balance and graduate students is multiple and possibly competing roles, such as being married. Mason and colleagues found that women were concerned about geographic location and conflicts with partners or spouses and children as reasons for not pursuing the professoriate.

Department and institutional culture plays a strong role in the literature on faculty and work–life balance. Culture is often cited as the main reason that more faculty and staff do not use family and medical leave policies (Thompson, Beauvais, & Lyness, 1999). Research indicates that a cultural stigma exists against faculty productivity and childrearing. Taking advantage of existing work–life policies would make the need for more balance visible to department colleagues. The perceived stigma also impacts graduate students, who are being socialized into disciplinary culture and faculty work. Multiple studies on female graduate students find a lack of role models and a perception that work–life balance and childrearing are incongruent with faculty success, especially for achieving tenure (Brus, 2006; Golde, 2000; Mason et al., 2009). Mason and colleagues (2009) noted:

> Forty-five percent of men and 39 percent of the women we surveyed indicated that they wanted to pursue careers as professors with research emphasis when they started their PhD programs, but only 36 percent of men and 27 percent of women stated that was their career goal at the time of the survey. (p. 14)

For female students, the reasons for deciding not to pursue an academic career are often directly connected to childrearing. Few female doctoral students see women faculty who have children at all; female faculty who do have children are often viewed as making significant sacrifices between parenting and work responsibilities (Brus, 2006; Ward & Wolf-Wendel, 2004). Role models are particularly important, as Mason and colleagues (2009) found that female graduate students who do not see women faculty with children are far less likely (12% to 46%) to rate research-intensive universities as family friendly. Moreover, graduate students are directly experiencing the demands of research and the cultural expectations of competitive departments. Brus (2006) notes that institutional expectations leave graduate students feeling as if they must be constantly available to faculty mentors. Brus concludes, "This expectation often translates into the necessity of students' spending sixty to eighty contact hours per week in their department merely to remain competitive" (p. 36).

The consequences of a lack of attention to work–life issues for graduate students are many. While not specifically about a work–life event, such as the birth of a child or medical issue, Golde's (2000) study on doctoral students indicates that a break or breach in a student's progress can be disruptive to his or her degree progress. Female students and students of color are more likely to experience disruptions that lead to attrition. Brus (2006) notes that attrition rates are higher for women and students of color as compared to their White counterparts. Brus (2006) reports:

> For the population [graduate students] I serve, issues of work–life balance are not only critical to successful completion of a graduate degree but also play a significant role in a woman's ability to remain competitive for important postdoctoral and tenure-track positions after graduation. (p. 34)

Another consequence of a lack of work–life balance for graduate students is a shift in career goals. Mason and colleagues (2009) found that graduate students who observed faculty with little to no work–life balance were more likely to change their career goals away from the professoriate. This trend is greater for female students who have, or desire to have, children. Beiber and Worley (2006) added to these findings by showing that some students observed professors who used the flexibility of faculty work to be engaged with family, as well as others, particularly those at research intensive universities, who seemed to work all the time.

Recommendations for Practice

The literature on work–life issues among graduate students points to a variety of significant issues that include demographic changes possibly related to increased family responsibilities, competitive department cultures, a lack of faculty role models who have balance, and a connection between work–life balance and retention. Institutions of higher education need to consider evaluating current policies and practices and developing new programs and policies to support graduate students. By doing so, graduate students are more likely to complete their graduate programs, become dedicated alumni, and, in some cases, enter the professoriate, a goal of many doctoral programs. Following are several recommendations for institutional leaders to consider.

Establish Family and Medical Leave for Graduate Students. The most important consideration for any campus that employs graduate students in a variety of paid positions is to establish a family and medical leave policy modeled after the federal Family and Medical Leave Act (FMLA). FMLA provides a number of job protections for employees who adopt or give birth to a child, have a serious medical condition, or have a family member with a serious medical condition (U.S. Department of Labor, 1993). The provisions of FMLA allow for up to six weeks of unpaid leave and a guarantee of an equivalent job upon returning to work. However, FMLA requires that employees have 12 months of employment at the organization and 1,250 hours worked in the 12 months preceding the leave.

A FMLA policy designed for graduate students should include several significant provisions, beginning with a definition of *family or medical event* that mirrors the federal FMLA. Most existing leave options for graduate students, including those noted next, are only for birth or adoption of a child. Not only do graduate students need leave for additional family or medical events, they also need job protections following a family or medical event. Graduate students are often not guaranteed their current position after returning to work. If they need to take a leave of absence, there are generally policies that allow for continued enrollment in degree programs, but no protections for the same or equivalent paid assistantship to continue upon returning from a leave. The eligibility criteria will also need to vary as graduate students work part-time and often for nine months, making them ineligible given the federal FMLA criteria. In addition, a family and medical leave policy should allow graduate students to take an absence from the university without losing university services, such as health insurance and library and e-mail access. Ideally, an institution would go beyond FMLA to include paid leave for at least six weeks. Frequently, the number of graduate students requiring such a leave is so small that institutions would not need significant funds to support such a policy. Two examples of family and medical leave policies related to graduate students are those at Princeton University and the University of California, Berkeley. These policies are available through the respective institutions' websites.

Provide Paid or Subsidized Health Insurance. Access to health insurance is a fundamental need for many graduate students. Mason and colleagues (2009) noted that access to health insurance was a major reason for concerns about having children while in graduate school. Access to health care among graduate students varies across states and university systems. Generally, graduate students who are receiving a paid assistantship will also have access to health insurance at a reduced cost. Graduate students may also have access to subsidized health care options regardless of their university employment status. While the implications of the Patient Protection and Affordable Care Act are still being realized for higher education, concerns are arising over access to health care. Students in the University of California system, a centralized health insurance system that is excluded under provisions in the Patient Protection and Affordable Care Act, have raised concerns over a loophole that allows for lifetime caps. Other states, such as New Jersey, that provide subsidized health insurance may see these programs phased out under the Patient Protection and Affordable Care Act, resulting in significantly higher premiums for graduate students. Colleges and universities need to consider the important role of health care and the need for graduate students to have access to subsidized coverage.

Create Lactation Rooms Across Campus. As noted in Rose's vignette at the beginning of this chapter, graduate students who are returning to school after birth of a child may require a private area with appropriate facilities, such as a sink and a lock on the door, to lactate. All too often, graduate students are put in shared offices, cubicles without privacy, or do not have access to an office. Without privacy, the ability to work as a teaching or research assistant is limited. Lactation rooms are required in most states for employees and can easily be opened for graduate student use. To allow for maximum flexibility on geographically large campuses, lactation rooms need to be in multiple locations, with those locations well documented on websites and in spaces frequented by graduate students. A few examples of campuses with multiple lactation rooms include the University of Illinois, Chicago and the University of Michigan.

Establish a Student Family Support Unit. The needs of students with families are many; one consequence is the challenge for each department or unit on a college campus to provide individually appropriate support. Establishing a university-wide unit on campus that facilitates a series of programs and services for graduate students with families can help to centralize services and may be more fiscally appropriate. These units often offer drop-in childcare to allow a graduate student to attend a lecture or an important department meeting. They may also offer a meeting space for student parent groups and a centralized electronic location for policies and services, and they may sponsor events related to eldercare, childrearing, and balancing the multiple expectations of graduate school. These resource centers do not require extensive staff or facilities but can be essential in supporting graduate students with work–life issues.

Michigan State University has a strong model for a program that supports undergraduate and graduate students with families. The Family Resource Center has a variety of efforts that support student parents, such as providing a physical space for meetings, maintaining a listserv, creating programs and events, outlining policies, connecting students to services across campus, and offering counseling services.

Evaluate Access to Childcare. A major concern for graduate students is access to high-quality childcare. While many institutions have created childcare centers on or near campuses, they often have limited capacity and therefore grant priority enrollment to faculty and staff. In my research on work–life balance, I found that campus-based childcare centers commonly had waitlists of over two years, did not offer infant care, and were unsubsidized with monthly costs beyond the financial reach of graduate students (Lester, 2013). College and universities need to evaluate not just the existence of childcare centers, but also the capacity and cost with attention to providing access to graduate student families. If that is not possible given the current fiscal climate, other options are childcare vouchers to be used at community childcare centers, paid access to online services such as Care .com or Sittercity.com, and organizing individual students and groups through a family resource center to share childcare responsibilities. Examples of voucher programs are the Graduate Student Senate Child Care

NEW DIRECTIONS FOR HIGHER EDUCATION • DOI:10.1002/he

Voucher Program at the University of Massachusetts, Amherst and the Grant for Childcare at Northern Arizona University.

Provide a Living Wage. Many of the issues related to health insurance and childcare result from a lack of access to the Family and Medical Leave Act as well as the wages paid to graduate students. Stipends for doctoral students vary dramatically across disciplines and geographic region. In 2008, *The Chronicle of Higher Education* surveyed 100 universities and found stipends that range from a little over $3,000 to $28,000, with significant differences across geographic location and academic discipline. For example, teaching assistant stipends in sociology are over $22,000 at New York University and $3,000 at North Dakota State University (Montell, 2008). While in some smaller cities or more rural areas a small stipend would constitute a living wage by federal standards, other areas have a cost of living that far exceeds graduate student stipends. As an example, a report by the Center for Urban Future found that the average monthly apartment rent in New York City is over $2,800, far more than San Francisco, another city with a high cost of living (Bowles, Kotkin, & Giles, 2009). Analyzing graduate student stipends with the potential for increasing their wages has direct benefits in more competitive graduate programs. Highly qualified students are more likely to receive multiple offers, compare their benefits package, and choose the university with the most lucrative package.

Create Department-Level Expectations for Hours Worked. Often, graduate students will work well beyond their required 20 hours per week to please their faculty supervisors and ensure that their assistantships continue (Brus, 2006). Departments and individual faculty need to be educated on the importance of fair employment practices to include tracking hours worked. Without doing so, a culture of competition and productivity will continue and may lead to certain graduate students, such as women, opting out of the professoriate to seek work–life balance. The impact of competitive cultures is well documented in the literature on faculty and graduate students (Fogg, 2003; Kerber, 2005; Mason & Goulden, 2004; Williams, 2000). Providing a supportive environment that allows for balance between graduate school and family (or life) has direct benefits for graduate student retention and success. Departments need to be sensitive to the fact that graduate students are constantly watching what faculty do with their time to make decisions about future career goals (Beiber & Worley, 2006).

Conclusion

Graduate students are an integral part of colleges and universities; they teach undergraduate courses, assist faculty in research projects, and work across a variety of academic and student affairs offices (Ampaw & Jaeger, 2012). Yet graduate students are often left out of the discussion of fair employment practices, because administrators assume that their needs are being met at the department level and through teaching and research assistantships.

Graduate student unions have questioned these assumptions, advocating for access to decent and affordable health care and childcare, an end to punitive fees, and better pay for the work done on campus. To work toward building graduate programs with fewer years to degrees and with higher graduate student retention, and to continue to build a vital alumni network, institutions need to turn their attention to their graduate students and consider their work–life needs. I do acknowledge that the recommendations outlined in this chapter require precious fiscal resources, but I challenge higher education institutions to consider the overall human and fiscal loss when graduate students either drop out of school altogether or remain in a doctoral program for eight or more years. The challenge for universities is to use innovative measures that support the crucial work and development of the graduate student population.

References

Ampaw, F. D., & Jaeger, A. J. (2012). Completing the three stages of doctoral education: An event history analysis. *Research in Higher Education, 53*(6), 640–660.

Armenti, C. (2004). May babies and posttenure babies: Maternal decisions of women professors. *Review of Higher Education, 27*(2), 211–231.

Beiber, J. P., & Worley, L. K. (2006). Conceptualizing the academic life: Graduate students' perceptions. *Journal of Higher Education, 77*(6), 1009–1035.

Bowles, J., Kotkin, J., & Giles, D. (2009). *Reviving the middle class dream in NYC.* Center for Urban Future. Retrieved from http://nycfuture.org/research/publications/reviving-the-middle-class-dream-in-nyc

Brus, C. P. (2006). Seeking balance in graduate school: A realistic expectation or a dangerous dilemma? In M. Guentzel & B. Nesheim (Eds.), *New Directions for Student Services: No. 115. Supporting graduate and professional students: The role of student affairs* (pp. 31–45). San Francisco, CA: Jossey-Bass.

Council of Graduate Schools (CGS). (2008). *Ph.D. completion and attrition: Analysis of baseline demographic data from the Ph.D. completion project.* Washington, DC: Author.

Curtis, J. W. (2004). Balancing work and family for faculty: Why it's important. *Academe Online, 90*(6). Retrieved from http://www.jstor.org/stable/40252701

Drago, R., Colbeck, C., Stauffer, K. D., Pirretti, A., Burkum, K., Fazioli, J. ... Habasevich, T. (2005). Bias against caregiving. *Academe, 91*(5), 22–25.

Finkel, S. K., Olswang, S., & She, N. (1994). Childbirth, tenure, and promotion for women faculty. *Review of Higher Education, 17*(3), 259–270.

Fogg, P. (2003, June 13). Family time: Why some women quit their coveted tenure-track jobs. *The Chronicle of Higher Education*, p. A10.

Golde, C. M. (2000). Should I stay or should I go? Student descriptions of the doctoral attrition process. *Review of Higher Education, 23*(2), 199–227.

Kerber, L. K. (2005, March 18). We must make the academic workplace more humane and equitable. *The Chronicle of Higher Education*, p. B6.

Lester, J. (2013). Organizational change for work–life balance. *Review of Higher Education, 36*(4), 463–488.

Lester, J., & Sallee, M. (Eds.). (2009). *Establishing the family-friendly campus: Best practices.* Sterling, VA: Stylus Publishing.

Mason, M. A., & Goulden, M. (2002). Do babies matter? The effect of family formation on the lifelong careers of academic men and women. *Academe, 88*(6), 21–27.

Mason, M. A., & Goulden, M. (2004). Do babies matter (Part II)? Closing the baby gap. *Academe, 90*(6), 10–15.

Mason, M. A., Goulden, M., & Frasch, K. (2009). Why graduate students reject the fast track: A study of thousands of doctoral students shows that they want balanced lives. *Academe, 95*(1), 11–16.

Monroe, K., Ozyurta, S., Wrigleya, T., & Alexander, A. (2008). Gender equality in academia: Bad news from the trenches, and some possible solutions. *Perspectives on Politics, 6,* 215–233.

Montell, G. (2008, December 2). Graduate students' pay and benefits vary widely, survey shows. *The Chronicle of Higher Education.* Retrieved from http://chronicle.com/blogs/onhiring/graduate-students-paybenefits-vary-widely-survey-shows/770

O'Meara, K., & Campbell, C. (2011). Faculty sense of agency in decisions about work and family. *Review of Higher Education, 34*(3), 447–476.

Sallee, M. (2011). The ideal worker or the ideal father: Organizational structures and culture in the gendered university. *Research in Higher Education, 53*(7), 782–802.

Sullivan, B., Hollenshead, C., & Smith, G. (2004). Developing and implementing work-family policies for faculty. *Academe, 90*(6), 24–27.

Thompson, C., Beauvais, L., & Lyness, K. (1999). When work–family benefits are not enough: The influence of work–family culture on benefit utilization. *Journal of Vocational Behavior, 54,* 392–415.

U.S. Department of Education. (2003). *Digest of Education Statistics.* Washington, DC: Author.

U.S. Department of Education. (2011). *Digest of Education Statistics.* Washington, DC: Author.

U.S. Department of Labor. (1993). *Family and Medical Leave Act.* Wage and Hour Division. Retrieved from www.dol.gov/whd/fmla/

Wagner, J. G. (2002). *Teaching the growing population of nontraditional students.* Reston, VA: National Business Education Association.

Ward, K., & Wolf-Wendel, L. (2004). Fear factor: How safe is it to make time for family? *Academe, 90*(6), 28–31.

Williams, J. C. (2000, October 27). How the tenure track discriminates against women. *The Chronicle of Higher Education.* Retrieved from http://chronicle.com/article/How-the-Tenure-Track/46312/

Williams, J. C. (2003, April 18). The subtle side of discrimination. *The Chronicle of Higher Education,* p. C5. Retrieved from http://chronicle.com/article/The-Subtle-Side-of/12547

Yoest, C. (2004, February). *Parental leave in academia.* Retrieved from www.faculty.virginia.edu/familyandtenure/

Younes, M. N., & Asay, S. M. (1998). Resilient women: How female graduate students negotiate their multiple roles. *College Student Journal, 32,* 451–462.

JAIME LESTER is associate professor of higher education at George Mason University.

6

Historically Black colleges and universities have long served as an important source for minority undergraduates who later go on to receive a doctoral degree.

The Impact of Historically Black Colleges and Universities on Doctoral Students

Joretta Joseph

Historically Black colleges and universities (HBCUs) continue to be important institutions of higher education where African American students are educated (Kim, 2002). HBCUs were founded with the purpose to educate newly freed slaves at a time when African Americans had very few educational options. As such, they are an institutional product of an era of socially constructed racism and discrimination against African Americans. Until the desegregation of public colleges in the early 1960s, HBCUs were the major avenue towards postsecondary degree attainment and a higher education for 90% of the African Americans who were enrolled in colleges and universities (Kim & Conrad, 2006). In areas of science, technology, engineering, and mathematics (STEM), these institutions continue to educate a significant number of African Americans towards a bachelor's degree, particularly those who go on to pursue graduate degrees in the STEM fields (Burrelli & Rapoport, 2008; Clewell, Cosentino de Cohen, & Tsui, 2010; Cross, 2001). Some researchers attribute this success to a supportive environment that stresses hands-on nurturing and engagement (Cross, 1997; Nelson Laird, Bridges, Morelon-Quainoo, Williams, & Salinas Holmes, 2007). This engagement begins from the time students walk onto an HBCU campus, where a community of faculty and staff are all invested in their well-being. Such a culture fosters an institutional and communal network that works to advance the opportunity of each student (Subramaniam & Wyer, 1998).

Beyond its function as a social and cultural foundation, a historically Black college or university offers additional value to its students. Jill Constantine (1994) found that HBCUs add economic market value to the students who attend those institutions. For example, in Constantine's study,

NEW DIRECTIONS FOR HIGHER EDUCATION, no. 163, Fall 2013 © Wiley Periodicals, Inc.
Published online in Wiley Online Library (wileyonlinelibrary.com) • DOI:10.1002/he.20066

students who attended a HBCU earned higher wages than those who attended other kinds of institutions. One explanation for such advantages might be in the academic curriculum offered by HBCUs, specifically the attention given to remedial instruction for those students who enter college with field-specific deficiencies. By offering remedial instruction to students, institutions signal their willingness to invest in the students' success over an extended period of time, while other institutions might adopt a "sink-or-swim" attitude with students (Constantine, 1994; Kim, 2002; Kim & Conrad, 2006). In addition to beneficial financial outcomes, increases to student self-concept and self-efficacy result from engagement within the HBCU environment. By comparing the increases in self-concept of African American students at historically Black and traditionally White institutions (TWIs), Berger and Milem (2000) found that HBCUs provide an educational environment that promotes unique positive academic outcomes. These outcomes are particularly notable since many of the students who attend HBCUs are not well prepared for college compared to their peers (Abelman & Dalessandro, 2009; Kim & Conrad, 2006) and are of a lower socioeconomic status than those who attend TWIs (Kim & Conrad, 2006; Wenglinsky, 1997).

The purpose of this chapter is to focus on the unique characteristics that make HBCUs effective educational environments for minority students, specifically in terms of science, technology, engineering, and mathematics (STEM) disciplines. In particular, I examine the organizational culture at HBCUs and consider what impact this culture has on underrepresented students who go on to pursue doctoral degrees in the STEM fields. Given the increased national emphasis to diversify the population of scholars pursuing advanced degrees in these areas, the role of historically Black colleges and universities is important to enhancing the educational pathway (Maton & Hrabowski, 2004; Maton, Pollard, Weise, & Hrabowski, 2012).

HBCUs: The Beginning for Many With PhDs in the STEM Fields

Historically Black colleges and universities have been the primary source of underrepresented minority students who attain STEM doctoral degrees (Burrelli & Rapoport, 2008). Even as the number of African Americans receiving bachelor's degrees from HBCUs has fallen, as more students attend other institutional types, historically Black institutions continue to provide an academic conduit for young scholars (Burrelli & Rapoport, 2008). In particular, such institutions provide beneficial advantages to women. As one example, nearly three-quarters of African American women who later received STEM doctorates completed their undergraduate degrees at HBCUs (Solórzano, 1995). Spelman College and Bennett College, both private HBCUs for female students, have long served as the origin for future doctorates. In the biological sciences, for instance, 73% of African American female doctorates from 1975 to 1992 received a HBCU baccalaureate; almost all of those women graduated from either Spelman or Bennett (Leggon & Pearson, 1997). These trends have continued into the 21st century. Research from Sibulkin and Butler (2011) documented that HBCUs comprise 70% of the origin institutions for African American doctoral-degree recipients in STEM from 2001 to 2005. Recent data from the National Science Foundation (NSF; 2012) suggests this trend has continued, with Howard University as the primary undergraduate origin institution for future minority doctorates.

Beyond their role in producing students who go on to doctoral degrees, HBCUs also serve a crucial function in terms of providing doctorates for minority students. As one example, Howard University, which is one of two HBCUs that is classified as a research institution, awarded its first doctorate degree in 1958 in the field of chemistry (Fields, 1998; Sibulkin & Butler, 2011). Howard is an important source of minority female doctorates, particularly in the areas of psychology and the life sciences (Sharpe & Swinton, 2012).

In short, attending a historically Black institution increases the likelihood that a student will pursue a doctoral degree at some point. Sibulkin and Butler (2011) explain one possible rationale: "HBCUs provide a more encouraging environment ... given the higher percentage of Black faculty and administrators as role models and the psychological advantages that accrue from being in the visible majority" (p. 848). Institutional factors such as peer support groups, networking opportunities, undergraduate research opportunities, and academic support services further the likelihood of student success (Perna et al., 2009).

HBCUs as Vehicles of Social Capital

Given their unique history, their role as the primary provider of undergraduate education to African Americans who attain doctoral degrees in the STEM fields, and their implicit social contract with African Americans, historically Black institutions are also a vehicle of social capital (Brown & Davis, 2001). Defined by its organizational function, social capital is the sum of social trust, individual behavior, and informal associative networks (Lappe & DuBois, 1997). At the most basic level, social capital enables a person to make choices beyond his or her perceived limits within society. For these choices to take place, social capital also inherently weaves the concepts of agency (power through knowledge), civic engagement, and new skill development (Lappe & DuBois, 1997). All of these elements are also inherent in the overall mission of HBCUs. This role is evident by the manner in which HBCUs emphasize the advantages of education to African Americans, their community, and the larger society.

Benjamin Mays, the social activist and former president of Morehouse College, reflected on this unique role thusly: "[HBCUs] should never exist in isolation … each individual must consider himself in relation to the social whole, the community, and the world" (1942, p. 403). An important goal of the HBCU curriculum is the idea of social responsibility and social development. This commitment has been known to increase self-image and confidence (Patterson, Dunston, & Daniels, 2013) and, consequently, academic achievement (Swail, Redd, & Perna, 2003). As Mays (1942) further noted, no stone is to be unturned in order to remove all obstacles that would not allow the best and finest students to succeed. HBCUs continue to perform this role and generate social capital by providing students an environment that encourages confidence, a sense of responsibility, strong formal and informal relations, and the capacity to create solutions and options beyond the individual (Allen, 1992; Brown & Davis, 2001; Fountaine, 2012; Kim & Conrad, 2006; Wenglinsky, 1997).

How do historically Black institutions encourage and support the academic, social, professional, and personal development of their students? Extant research has documented the unique role of the institutional climate at HBCUs (Berger & Milem, 2000), particularly in terms of promoting a positive academic outcome for the student. From the time of initial enrollment, students at HBCUs experience a community of faculty and staff who are invested in their well-being and success. In this way, the institutional climate is the result of a broader network that operates to advance the opportunity of each student (Perna et al., 2009; Subramaniam & Wyer, 1998). The interactions with faculty, staff, and peers are invaluable because of their support and encouragement (Fries-Britt & Turner, 2002). This developmentally powerful environment provides students with a sense of psychological well-being and cultural affinity, while also nurturing academic and social relations that could last for many years beyond the undergraduate college experience (Kim, 2002; Subramaniam & Wyer, 1998). This connection between a welcoming environment and academic success is also noted by the College Board (2008), which suggests that institutions are best served by concentrating on the academic needs and challenges of low-income, minority, and first-generation students who are more likely to drop out (Allen, 1992; College Board, 2008).

The relationships between the students and faculty may be at the heart of what makes historically Black institutions successful in terms of their students' academic and social achievements. The interactions between the two are essential to the students' participation in social groups, academic organizations, and student government as well as to the development of a positive self-concept (Berger & Milem, 2000). Research conducted by the American Association of University Professors (1995) suggested that the relationships between faculty and students at HBCUs show that faculty have a genuine concern for the students' well-being via true support and understanding. Students from HBCUs report that faculty are sensitive to their needs, notice their talents, closely mentor them, encourage them to attend graduate school, and care for each of them as a unique individual, not just another student (Fountaine, 2012; Joseph, 2007; Perna et al., 2009). This relationship is of particular importance since faculty stipulate what is anticipated from their students in and outside of the classroom via their demeanor, expectations, and curriculum (Perna et al., 2009; Suarez-Balcazar, Orellana-Damacela, Portillo, Rowan, & Andrews-Guillen, 2003). Such relationships have been associated with positive college adjustment and the development of a strong racial identity (Hinderlie & Kenny, 2002; Joseph, 2007).

Students have described peer relationships at HBCUs as their "saving grace" (Fries-Britt, Younger, & Hall, 2010). Establishing peer relationships allows for a sense of community and the ability to fit in socially, both of which strengthen a student's ability to persist towards graduation. Peers are also an important support system. A peer-to-peer relationship encourages each student and allows each to express her or his concerns. This characteristic is important because having a sense of communal belonging is a central characteristic to self-confidence, itself a critical attribute towards succeeding in graduate school (Herzig, 2004; Phinney, 1990; Swail, Redd, & Perna, 2003).

Understanding Pathways from HBCUs to Doctoral Education

When considering the success of historically Black institutions in educating minority students who go on to achieve doctoral degrees, other institutional types can learn valuable lessons. For example, Brazziel and Brazziel (1997) suggest that a dedicated faculty, an abundance of role models, committed efforts towards mentoring, and student engagement with alumni as well as industry contacts are all important preparatory efforts towards eventually succeeding in a graduate curriculum. Beyond these more visible institutional efforts, however, the authors propose that success in key academic disciplines such as mathematics offers a foundation for academic development. As other chapters in this volume have suggested, early efforts to socialize minority students into academic norms of specific disciplines can result in productive outcomes related to diversity in doctoral education. It is not enough to simply provide access; rather, postsecondary institutions should consider how minority students experience the curriculum and if such experiences empower students toward future degree attainment.

By gaining substantial research experience in the disciplines, minority students are well prepared to make the transition to a doctoral program and understand the challenges of research practice. Tsui (2007) concluded, "There is considerable evidence from multiple research studies to suggest that engaging in hands-on research ... is an effective strategy for increasing the number who pursue [doctoral] degrees" (p. 559). Programs such as the NSF's HBCU-UP support research opportunities for undergraduate students at historically Black institutions, particularly in the STEM disciplines. The goal of such opportunities is to facilitate diversity in doctoral education by broadening the pathways towards participation from the time of undergraduate studies.

Examples do exist of partnerships between historically Black institutions and traditional White campuses that provide a bridge from undergraduate to graduate studies. For example, the partnership between Fisk University (a private HBCU in Nashville, Tennessee) and Vanderbilt University (a private research university, also in Nashville) supports a Master's to PhD Bridge Program. The program focuses on astronomy, physics, biology, chemistry, and materials science, and encourages minority students enrolled in the master's program at Fisk to work in collaboration with Vanderbilt faculty. Students receive full funding and a strong academic foundation at Fisk, both of which prepare them for admission into the doctoral program at Vanderbilt. Program cornerstones include peer mentors from both campuses, faculty mentors from both campuses, research opportunities that allow students to work with cross-institutional resources, and professional development seminars designed to prepare students for doctoral programs (Stassun et al., 2011). Table 6.1 summarizes a selection of bridge programs between HBCUs and other institutional types, emphasizing those components that facilitate the success of underrepresented minority doctoral students.

Students progress through their graduate education with varying degrees of prior knowledge, skills, and contacts (Gardner & Holley, 2011). The graduate school experience is not the same for all students. For students of color, the norms and values of the department and discipline may not fit the cultural diversity of their background or their lifestyles (Gardner & Holley, 2011). In addition, a student's success in an undergraduate curriculum does not guarantee his or her success in a doctoral program. Colleges and universities would be well served to consider the unique variations across institutions, disciplines, and departments when developing plans to ensure that underrepresented students thrive in doctoral education. As one example, doctoral students are typically expected to identify a faculty mentor early in the program of study and develop a coherent research agenda that aligns with the advisor and the discipline. For students who completed a bachelor's degree at a HBCU, the lack of diverse faculty role models or the different cultural norms between HBCUs and other institutional types might be disorienting (Joseph, 2007).

Conclusion

In this chapter, I illustrated the unique cultural environment of historically Black colleges and universities and outlined how those advantages benefit minority students as they move into a doctoral program. For a graduate student to be successful, the student must be able to navigate through the

Table 6.1. Summary of HBCU Partnership Bridge and Related Programs

Program	HBCU Partner	Other Partners	Target Disciplines	Program Components
Bridges to the Doctorate Program	Alcorn State University	Penn State University	Veterinary and biomedical sciences	Stipend, tuition benefits, mentorship, shared curriculum
Master's to PhD Bridge Program	Fisk University	Vanderbilt University	Physics, astronomy, material science	Financial support, mentorship, shared research opportunities, support groups
HBCU-UP ACE (funded by NSF, at multiple locations)	Southern A&M University	Bejing Forestry University, Oak Ridge Laboratories	Sustainable materials, energy, technology	Collaborative research opportunities, internships, international collaboration
UC–HBCU Initiative	Florida A&M University	University of California, Santa Barbara	Education, evaluation, assessment	Financial support, travel support, mentorship, research opportunities

academic demands, departmental values, faculty perceptions, and institutional norms. Since HBCUs graduate a significant number of underrepresented students who later receive the doctorate, researchers and practitioners have much to learn about the formative experiences provided by historically Black institutions. Their prominence signals not only their importance within the higher education system and the contribution they make to diversity, but also the ability for other kinds of institutions to learn from and engage with the unique HBCU cultural environment.

References

Abelman, R., & Dalessandro, A. (2009). The institutional vision of historically Black colleges and universities. *Journal of Black Studies, 40*(2), 106–124.

Allen, W. R. (1992). The color of success: African-American college student outcomes at predominantly White and historically Black public colleges and universities. *Harvard Educational Review, 62*(1), 26–44.

American Association of University Professors. (1995). The historically black colleges and universities: A future in the balance. *Academe, 81*(1), 49–57.

Berger, J., & Milem, J. F. (2000). Exploring the impact of historically Black colleges in promoting the development of undergraduates' self-concept. *Journal of College Student Development, 41*(4), 381–394.

Brazziel, W., & Brazziel, M. (1997). Distinctives of high producers of minority science and engineering doctoral starts. *Journal of Science Education and Technology, 6*(2), 143–153.

Brown, M. C., II, & Davis, J. E. (2001). The historically Black college as social contract, social capital, and social equalizer. *Peabody Journal of Education, 76*(1), 31–49.

Burrelli, J. S., & Rapoport, A. (2008). *Role of HBCUs and baccalaureate-origin institutions of Black S&E doctorate recipients.* Washington, DC: National Science Foundation.

Clewell, B. C., Cosentino de Cohen, C., & Tsui, L. (2010). *Capacity building to diversity STEM: Realizing potential among HBCUs.* Washington, DC: Urban Institute.

College Board. (2008). *Coming to our senses: Education and the American future.* Retrieved from http://professionals.collegeboard.com/profdownload/coming-to-our-senses -college-board-2008.pdf

Constantine, J. (1994). The added value of historically Black colleges. *Academe, 80*(3), 12–17.

Cross, T. E. (1997). A bold effort to measure the nurturing environment at Black colleges and universities. *Journal of Blacks in Higher Education, 17,* 49–51.

Cross, T. E. (2001). Two historically Black colleges show greater Ph.D. productivity than do Dartmouth, Emory, Vanderbilt and the University of Michigan. *Journal of Blacks in Higher Education, 34,* 122–126.

Fields, C. D. (1998). Black scientists: A history of exclusion. *Black Issues in Higher Education, 3*(15), 12–16.

Fountaine, T. (2012). The impact of faculty–student interaction on Black doctoral students attending historically Black institutions. *Journal of Negro Education, 81*(2), 136–147.

Fries-Britt, S., & Turner, B. (2002). Uneven stories: Successful Black collegians on a Black and a White campus. *Review of Higher Education, 25*(3), 315–330.

Fries-Britt, S., Younger, T., & Hall, W. (2010). Lessons from high-achieving students of color in physics. In S. R. Harper & C. B. Newman (Eds.), *New Directions for Institutional Research: No. 148. Students of color in STEM* (pp. 75–83). San Francisco, CA: Jossey-Bass.

Gardner, S. K., & Holley, K. (2011). "Those invisible barriers are real": The progression of first-generation students through doctoral education. *Equity & Excellence in Education, 44*(1), 77–92.

Herzig, A. H. (2004). Becoming mathematics: Women and students of color choosing and leaving doctoral mathematics. *Review of Educational Research, 74*(2), 171–214.

Hinderlie, H. H., & Kenny, M. (2002). Attachment, social support, and college adjustment among Black students at predominantly White universities. *Journal of College Student Development, 43*(3), 327–340.

Joseph, J. (2007). *The experiences of African American graduate students: A cultural transition* (Unpublished dissertation). University of Southern California, Los Angeles.

Kim, M. M. (2002). Historically Black vs. White institutions' academic development among Black students. *Review of Higher Education, 25*(4), 385–407.

Kim, M. M., & Conrad, C. F. (2006). The impact of historically Black colleges and universities on the academic success of African-American students. *Research in Higher Education, 47*(4), 399–427.

Lappe, F. M., & DuBois, P. M. (1997). Building social capital without looking backward. *National Civic Review, 86*(2), 119–128.

Leggon, C. B., & Pearson, W. J. (1997). The baccalaureate origins of African American female Ph.D. scientists. *Journal of Women and Minorities in Science and Engineering, 3*(4), 213–224.

Maton, K., & Hrabowski, F. (2004). Increasing the number of African American PhDs in the sciences and engineering: A strengths-based approach. *American Psychologist, 59*, 629–654.

Maton, K., Pollard, S., Weise, T., & Hrabowski, F. (2012). Meyerhoff Scholars Program: A strengths-based, institution-wide approach to increasing diversity in science, technology, engineering, and mathematics. *Mount Sinai Journal of Medicine, 79*(5), 610–623.

Mays, B. E. (1942). The role of the Negro liberal arts college in post-war reconstruction. *Journal of Negro Education, 11*(3), 400–411.

National Science Foundation. (2012). *Science and engineering indicators for 2012.* Arlington, VA: Author.

Nelson Laird, T., Bridges, B., Morelon-Quainoo, C., Williams, J., & Salinas Holmes, M. (2007). African American and Hispanic student engagement at minority serving and predominantly White institutions. *Journal of College Student Development, 48*(1), 39–56.

Patterson, G., Dunston, Y., & Daniels, K. (2013). Extreme makeover: Preserving the HBCU mission through service learning pedagogy. *Journal of African American Studies, 17*(2), 154–161.

Perna, L. W., Lundy-Wagner, V., Drezner, N., Gasman, M., Yoon, S., Bose, E., & Gary, L. (2009). The contribution of HBCUs to the preparation of African American women for STEM careers: A case study. *Research in Higher Education, 50*(1), 1–23.

Phinney, J. (1990). Ethnic identity in adolescents and adults: Review of research. *Psychological Bulletin, 108*(3), 499–514.

Sharpe, R., & Swinton, O. (2012). Beyond anecdotes: A quantitative examination of Black women in academe. *Review of Black Political Economy, 39*(3), 341–352.

Sibulkin, A., & Butler, J. S. (2011). Diverse colleges of origins of African American doctoral recipients, 2001–2005: Historically Black colleges and universities and beyond. *Research in Higher Education, 52*(8), 830–852.

Solórzano, D. (1995). The doctorate production and baccalaureate origins of African Americans in the sciences and engineering. *Journal of Negro Education, 64*(1), 15–32.

Stassun, K., Sturm, S., Holley-Bockelman, K., Burger, A., Ernst, D., & Webb, D. (2011). The Fisk-Vanderbilt Master's to Ph.D. Program: Recognizing, enlisting, and cultivating unrealized or unrecognized potential in underrepresented minority students. *American Journal of Physics, 79*(4), 374–379.

Suarez-Balcazar, Y., Orellana-Damacela, L., Portillo, N., Rowan, J., & Andrews-Guillen, C. (2003). Experiences of differential treatment among college students of color. *Journal of Higher Education, 74*(4), 428–444.

Subramaniam, B., & Wyer, M. (1998). Assimilating the "culture of no culture" in science: Feminist intervention in (de)mentoring graduate women. *Feminist Teacher, 12*(1), 12–28.

Swail, W., Redd, K., & Perna, L. W. (2003). *Retaining minority students in higher education.* San Francisco, CA: Jossey-Bass.

Tsui, L. (2007). Effective strategies to increase diversity in STEM fields: A review of the literature. *Journal of Negro Education, 76*(4), 555–581.

Wenglinsky, H. (1997). *Students at historically Black colleges and universities: Their aspirations & accomplishments.* Princeton, NJ: Educational Testing Service.

JORETTA JOSEPH is the program administrator and graduate advisor for the National Physical Science Consortium.

NEW DIRECTIONS FOR HIGHER EDUCATION • DOI:10.1002/he

7

Minority doctoral students at elite and highly competitive private research universities encounter distinctive challenges that can impact persistence, time to degree, and professional outcomes.

The Experiences of Minority Doctoral Students at Elite Research Institutions

Eva Graham

Science and engineering professions are segments of the U.S. workforce that rely heavily on the attainment of advanced degrees. These professions have become the subject of national dialogue and a source of concern in recent decades (Tsui, 2007). In particular, concern has been expressed over the potential of higher education to generate the number of advanced degree recipients needed to fulfill economic demands and who also reflect the diversity of American population (Sommers & Franklin, 2012). If the increase in the numbers of female and/or ethnic minority citizens is taken into consideration, the greatest pool of individuals able to generate the number of advanced degrees needed are women and underrepresented minorities. Population data from 2000–2008 showed a steady increase in the numbers of females by approximately 5 million each year over males and a steady increase in numbers of single-race, non-Hispanic, and Hispanic populations who were not White over that of those identified with White as one race (U.S. Census Bureau, 2011). In spite of this population growth, women and minorities remain underrepresented in science, technology, engineering, and mathematics (STEM) disciplines.

This chapter seeks to provide insight and potential solutions for the challenges that underrepresented minority graduate students in STEM disciplines often experience at elite private research institutions. It focuses on institutional challenges with matriculation, time to degree, attrition, and a lack of career satisfaction and persistence. The term "private elite" is given to universities that are not primarily funded through public monies and are regarded as having prestigious academic programs. The status of these programs attracts the best and most qualified faculty and students in the world. Of the 2,803 private institutions in the United States that existed in 2008,

New Directions for Higher Education, no. 163, Fall 2013 © Wiley Periodicals, Inc.
Published online in Wiley Online Library (wileyonlinelibrary.com) • DOI:10.1002/he.20067

fewer than 40 were considered "very high research institutions" or "elite" (National Center for Education Statistics, 2008). The most well-known U.S. institutions in this category are the Ivy League universities. There are eight highly selective universities commonly associated with the Ivy League system (Brown, Columbia, Cornell, Dartmouth, Harvard, Pennsylvania, Princeton, and Yale). The elite universities referred to in this chapter are not necessarily members of the Ivy League but have reputations for being highly selective in terms of student admission, as well as producing the largest numbers of Nobel laureates, spin-off companies, transferable technologies, and commercial patents. Stanford University, the Massachusetts Institute of Technology, and the California Institute of Technology are considered among those listed as private elite universities.

At Issue

Though drawn by the numerous and varied benefits offered by an elite education, many graduate students who are traditionally underrepresented in STEM disciplines experience feelings of isolation, lack of clarity around the process to degree, and campus cultures that foster extremely competitive academic environments (Museus, Palmer, Davis, & Maramba, 2011; Palmer, Maramba, & Gasman, 2012). These issues negatively impact their success in graduate school as well as their overall career satisfaction and persistence.

Extant research suggests that a diverse student population enhances the learning experiences of all students. Bertschinger (2012) concluded, "Excellence without diversity is orphan and diversity without excellence is destitute" (p. 54). In their work describing the consequences of considering race and ethnicity in the admission process, William Bowen and Derek Bok provide solid evidence that diversity enriches the educational experiences of all student communities on campus. They make an informed plea for institutions to create access for underrepresented minority students, especially private elite and Ivy League universities (Bowen & Bok, 2000). Their work also highlights the success of many minority graduates of top research institutions, further validating the value of minority students. The responsibility for campus diversity begins from the work of senior leadership in ensuring a campus climate that is supportive and conducive to student success.

Knowledge of the Process. Logic suggests that in order to increase the numbers of minority doctoral recipients, there must be increased access. However, if admitted students do not matriculate, the challenge of increasing the numbers of conferred doctorates remains a struggle even as the pool of qualified applicants continues to grow. It has been my experience that many recruitment challenges for an elite program can be attributed to the applicants' understanding of the process and the numbers of actual matriculates.

NEW DIRECTIONS FOR HIGHER EDUCATION • DOI:10.1002/he

The admission process is unique for every academic system. Private elites and top research universities often offer institutionally funded opportunities for potential students to visit campus. There is also the expectation that an applicant will research, and then contact, the faculty (or postdoctoral fellows) in the respective academic department. Understanding what is expected in order to gain admission can be as challenging as making the initial transition into a very competitive research program. A candidate's choice to matriculate can be influenced by many factors. For example, the level of education of either a parent or guardian is one factor that offers great insight into what an applicant understands about the admission process (Holley & Gardner, 2012).

Mullen, Goyette, and Soares (2003) compared and contrasted the influences of race, gender, and age along with parental and/or guardian levels of education on graduate school matriculation. When undergraduate institutional mission, selectivity, funding profile (private or public), and reputation (elite or research focused) were controlled for (thus controlling for individual preparation), the outcomes indicated that parental levels of education did have varying levels of influence on graduate school matriculation. Specifically, every year of parental education correlated directly to the positive potential for an individual's attainment of a doctorate (Mullen, Goyette, & Soares, 2003). This study supports the idea that an individual's understanding of the challenges, his or her willingness to make the personal and professional sacrifices required, and the availability of support are related to factors external to the student.

Departmental administration and potential faculty advisors are also a crucial aspect of the graduate experience. Knowledgeable administrators can help support an application during the admissions process and guide admitted students with advice. One of the most influential factors on the admission of underrepresented minorities is securing financial support for coursework and research. Elite campuses can have large endowments that allow for greater internal financial assistance; these endowments are managed by administrators. The potential exists for real and symbolic commitments to diversity in doctoral education through the application of financial resources (Crisp, Nora, & Taggart, 2009; Eagan, Hurtado, & Chang, 2010).

Time to Degree and Attrition. Underrepresented students must be prepared to make choices that will impact their entire graduate careers. Beyond financial aid and other institutional support systems, the campus culture is important to a student's success (Tierney, 1999). Tierney further suggests that individuals' security in their own cultural identity ultimately increases their potential for success. It has been my experience that for underrepresented minority students, the faculty advisor and other mentors influence their responses to environmental and academic pressures. Negative relationships can extend the time to degree or support a decision to leave the doctoral program.

New Directions for Higher Education • DOI:10.1002/he

A candidate's potential for success is definitely a consideration of a graduate selection committee. The progression from undergraduate to doctoral education can be a difficult transition, regardless of one's previous success. Faculty expectations are highly influenced by the culture of the institution, the individual laboratory and department, as well as the discipline itself, the graduate community of a campus, and that of the laboratory environment (Golde, 2005). Data from the Council on Graduate Schools (Sowell, Bell, & Zhang, 2008) indicated that the most successful graduate students (those who graduated within the average number of years for their respective programs) benefited from the following opportunities:

- Research presentations
- Publishing
- Access to information on career, mental, and physical health
- Networking and professional affiliations
- Mentorship
- Positive relationship with advisor(s)

Taking advantage of the opportunities provided by a well-funded program is difficult or almost impossible when a student is struggling with issues that are not being addressed. Gifted and talented minority students face unique challenges once admitted to programs where most of the students are from majority backgrounds. It may not be possible to eliminate all areas of hostility on a campus or in an off-campus community. However, the institution's student and academic affairs programming units can offer community building and counseling opportunities that can make a difference in a student's ability to work through very competitive and isolating academic environments that foster and often perpetuate disenfranchising experiences.

Knowledge of the Path to Graduation. The decision to admit a student at an elite research university is often made by departmental faculty and can depend on the funding available to support the individual. Administrative officers can support applications if they have the dual role of research faculty and administrator. Their influence will be otherwise limited if the institution ascribes to a process in which the faculty make admissions and academic decisions. Knowing this information can be helpful when a student needs financial advocacy, encounters academic obstacles, or faces conflict with one or more advisors or committee members. Underrepresented minority students should also be aware of the average number of hours per week and the average number of years typical graduate students will spend in their respective departments. A clear understanding of the expectation for qualifying and candidacy exams makes a difference in a student's ability to prepare for these academic milestones as well as tailor his or her academic endeavors accordingly (Nerad & Miller, 1996).

NEW DIRECTIONS FOR HIGHER EDUCATION • DOI:10.1002/he

Advisor Selection and Laboratory Groups. The selection of a research advisor is one of the most important decisions a student will make as part of a doctoral program. The relationship between graduate students and faculty is critical to designing a research agenda that leads to academic growth and professional advancement following graduation (Vasquez et al., 2006). Keeping the ultimate goal of graduating with the approval of a chosen advisor and getting a strong professional reference in mind, it has been my experience that underrepresented minority students often select the most comfortable and/or bearable lab environment. Strong competition exists for membership in groups of highly respected, renowned scholars (Campbell & Denes, 2000; Etzkowitz, Kemelgor, Nueschatz, & Uzzi, 2000). When possible, minority students should take the time needed to connect with more than one group with which they share research interests. They should also take the time to explore the potential for collaboration across departments. Web pages and publications are a first step towards identifying collaborators.

Underrepresented minority students should ultimately consider the selection of an advisor as the key to a future in the field of interest. It is important that time is given to fully investigate the potential for each relationship (Rutledge, Carter-Veale, & Tull, 2011). If the student provides the advisor an opportunity to bridge relationships with other research groups, he or she will be only more attractive and seen as a future asset to the group. Selecting an advisor based on available funding or the expectation that there will be a nurturing relationship can be a mistake. The most famous faculty can have many competing interests and thus be the most absent. This absence can leave the fate of a student's research in the hands of a postdoctoral fellow or lab manager, who is often even more invested in getting the approval of the same advisor.

The Role of the Mentor. Graduate students who seek mentorship within and outside of their departments have the opportunity to overcome the impacts of isolation (Davis & Warfield, 2011). It is important to recognize that there are academicians who understand the importance of mentoring the next generation and for whom it would be an honor to mentor a promising graduate student. Seeking group support through on-campus programs (often sponsored by offices in Student Affairs) and professional research groups can also have a positive impact on a graduate student's experience by offering necessary examples of professionals who have achieved the work and personal life balance to which many graduate students aspire.

Female graduate students who identify with an ethnic or racial minority population exist in a unique dual role. Many female students of color struggle with overt bias, an elusive career balance, the desire to start a family, the challenges of career development, and the perceived need to constantly prove themselves (Jones & Shorter-Gooden, 2003). As such, the intersection of race and gender can present greater challenges for supportive

NEW DIRECTIONS FOR HIGHER EDUCATION • DOI:10.1002/he

mentoring relationships. A recent study conducted by Moss-Racusin, Dovidio, Brescoll, Graham, and Handelsman (2012) produced clear evidence of bias in the practices of hiring laboratory managers in STEM graduate programs. In their randomized double-blind study, 127 chemistry, biology, and physics faculty at three public and three private universities were given profiles of applicants for laboratory manager positions. Candidate profiles were randomly assigned genders, and all were considered "qualified" with each having publication experience. When presented with the options of hiring female or male graduate students of equal qualification based on competence, salary, and the amount of mentoring they would be willing to give, faculty (regardless of gender) chose male students. Such studies raise questions regarding the impact of bias on a woman of color's self-esteem and her decision to persist in her chosen field (Moss-Racusin et al., 2012).

Continued existence of gender bias in STEM disciplines has a negative impact on access by female students to opportunities in the laboratory and ultimately in research groups. Those experiences can drive feelings of inadequacy that become very difficult to overcome. Early evidence of the "imposter syndrome" was shown in the work of Clance and Imes in 1978. Later research by Reybold and Alamia (2008) showed the extent to which the imposter syndrome can impact an individual's development and his or her ultimate contribution to the academic profession. The effects that the imposter phenomenon has on graduate students, who are often battling their own feelings of insecurity and difficult academic relationships, can be devastating.

The lack of minority representation in the STEM disciplines will certainly impact a minority student's ability to work with an advisor who understands the student's situation, background, and potential obstacles. However, I have had the good fortune to meet, interact with, and get to know majority faculty of all gender identities who respect and ultimately advocate for the greater good of their graduate students regardless of race or ethnicity.

Professional Experiences. Professional associations provide a supportive community and afford students an opportunity to build an encouraging research network beyond that of the laboratory or the institution. However, it should be clearly understood that presenting academic work at research conferences requires the approval of the advisor or principal investigator (PI). Being chosen to share work reflective of the research group can be an opportunity to exhibit expertise and attract potential postdoctoral fellowships or corporate or industry support. There are three main formats by which a student can share his or her work: poster sessions, oral presentations, and participating as a panelist on a subject or under a common theme.

Multiple advantages exist for each opportunity. Poster sessions provide an open and often less intimidating environment for first-time presenters or individuals doing work in a new area of research, while panel discussions allow scholars to interact with peers in a shared research area. The opportunity to engage with peers as well as the general audience can provide validation as well as ideas that lead to new and innovative directions for future work. The importance of both positive and critical feedback allows students to conceptualize their work in different ways that resonate with the disciplinary community. I provide in Table 7.1 an overview of conferences in the United States where graduate students and postdoctoral fellows are most certainly welcome and in my experience often encouraged to participate; these conferences usually award travel scholarships to doctoral students.

Concluding Thoughts

If the value of a graduate degree from an institution is measured against the contributions of its degree holder's success, then the strength of character of that graduate must also be measured by the challenges overcome to earn the degree. "One can achieve diversity and excellence by simply valuing people," concluded Bertschinger (2012, p. 55), who further noted that "accepting the premise of diversity and inclusion is one thing … achieving it is another" (p. 56). Bertschinger's remarks are drawn from his experience as a department head and professor of theoretical physics at the Massachusetts Institute of Technology (MIT). He goes on to report,

> For a number of years, women hovered around 30% of our graduating seniors. Last year [2012], however, we had 36 female graduates, or 38% of the total. For comparison, women were 45% of all MIT graduating seniors and approximately 21% of physics graduates nationwide. (p. 57)

MIT's record with underrepresented populations is equally successful. Bertschinger noted that in the same graduating class, the numbers of minority students went from 12% to 13% of undergraduates in STEM and 0 to 11% of those earning doctorates. Such efforts began by engaging department faculty in the work of recruiting, retaining, and graduating a diverse student population.

Bertschinger also worked with professional associations such as the American Physical Society (APS) to help colleagues understand the national challenges facing women and minorities in physics. Collectively, these endeavors demonstrate that challenges facing underrepresented minority doctoral students at elite private research institutions exist not just on a single campus or with a single student group. The efforts helped create a community focused on finding solutions rather than placing blame (emphasizing that all scientists love a good problem to solve). Bertschinger's (2012) final advice for department heads seeking positive change: "Think strategically, present a vision, and make the gain personal by showing colleagues what is in it for them" (p. 56).

NEW DIRECTIONS FOR HIGHER EDUCATION • DOI:10.1002/he

Table 7.1. Graduate Student Presentation Opportunities by Host Organization and Conference Season

Organization	Acronym	Target Audience	Website	Conference Season
Society of Women Engineers	SWE	Women Engineers	www.swe.org	Fall
American Association of University Women	AAUW	College/ University Women	www.aauw.org	Spring
American Geophysical Union	AGU	Earth and Space Scientists	www.agu.org	Winter
National Society of Black Engineers	NSBE	African American Engineers	www.nsbe.org	Winter/ Spring
Society of Hispanic Professional Engineers	SHPE	Hispanic Engineers	www.shpe.org	Spring
National Organization for the Advancement of Black Chemists and Chemical Engineers	NOBCChE	African American Chemists and Chemical Engineers	www.nobcche.org	Spring
American Educational Research Association	AERA	Educators and Faculty	www.AERA.org	Fall
National Science Teachers Association	NSTA	Science Educators and Science Teachers	www.nsta.org	Spring
National Association for Multicultural Education Administrators	NAMEPA	Minority Engineering Program Administrators	www.NAMEPA.org	Spring
Hispanic Associations of Colleges and Universities	HACU	Hispanic College Students, Staff, and Faculty	www.hacu.org	Fall
American Society for Engineering Educators	ASEE	Engineering Educators and Engineering Faculty	www.asee.org	Spring
American Association for the Advancement of Science	AAAS	Educators, Researchers and Scientists	www.aaas.org	Winter

Association on Higher Education and Disability	AHEAD	Educators and Disability Specialists	www.ahead.org	Summer
Annual Biomedical Research Conference for Minority Students	ABRCMS	Minority Students Conduction STEM Research	www.ABRCMS.org	Fall
American Indian Society for Engineering and Science	AISES	Native American Science and Engineering Students	www.aises.org	Fall
Society for the Advancement of Chicanos and Native Americans in Science	SACNAS	Chicano, Latino, and Native American Science Students	www.sacnas.org	Fall

Source: This list was compiled from several different sources, including the American Chemical Society, National Association for the Advancement of Black Chemists and Chemical Engineers, Hispanic Association of College and Universities, and others, although the final selection was based on the author's association and past participation.

For populations of high-achieving underrepresented minority students who choose STEM doctoral programs at elite private research institutions, taking advantage of institutional resources and administrative support can make the difference in their ability to translate a graduate experience into a successful career. While impacted by such factors as parental education and undergraduate preparation, an individual's success is not limited by those factors. It is equally important to understand that the most successful students can have the greatest challenges with self-esteem and efficacy. The very nature of "trailblazing" requires one to deal with making decisions and accepting mistakes as an integral part of the process.

References

Bertschinger, E. (2012). Advancing diversity and excellence in physics. *Physics @MIT Annual Journal, 2012,* 54–59. Retrieved from http://web.mit.edu/physics/news /physicsatmit/physicsatmit_12_bertschinger.pdf

Bowen, W. G., & Bok, D. (2000). *The shape of the river.* Princeton, NJ: Princeton University Press.

Campbell, G., & Denes, R. (2000). *Access denied: Race, ethnicity, and the scientific enterprise.* New York, NY: Oxford University Press.

Clance, P. R., & Imes, S. A. (1978). The imposter phenomenon in high achieving women: Dynamics and therapeutic interventions. *Psychotherapy: Theory, Research and Practice, 15*(8), 241–247.

Crisp, G., Nora, A., & Taggart, A. (2009). Student characteristics, pre-college, college, and environmental factors as predictors for majoring in and earning a STEM degree: An analysis of students attending a Hispanic serving institution. *Educational Researcher, 46*(4), 924–942.

Davis, D., & Warfield, M. (2011). The importance of networking in the academic and professional experiences of racial minority students in the USA. *Educational Research and Evaluation, 17*(2), 97–113.

Eagan, K., Hurtado, S., & Chang, M. (2010, November). *What matters in STEM: Institutional contexts that influence STEM bachelor's degree completion rates.* Paper presented at the Association for the Study of Higher Education annual meeting, Indianapolis, IN.

Etzkowitz, H., Kemelgor, C., Nueschatz, M., & Uzzi, B. (2000). *Athena unbound: The advancement of women in science and technology.* Cambridge, MA: Cambridge University Press.

Golde, C. (2005). The role of the department and discipline in doctoral student attrition: Lessons from four departments. *Journal of Higher Education, 76*(6), 669–700.

Holley, K., & Gardner, S. (2012). Navigating the pipeline: How socio-cultural influences impact first-generation doctoral students. *Journal of Diversity in Higher Education, 5*(2), 112–121.

Jones, C., & Shorter-Gooden, K. (2003). *Shifting.* New York, NY: HarperCollins.

Moss-Racusin, C., Dovidio, J., Brescoll, V., Graham, M., & Handelsman, J. (2012). Science faculty's subtle gender biases favor male students. *PNAS.* Retrieved from www.pnas.org/content/early/2012/09/14/1211286109.short

Mullen, A., Goyette, K., & Soares, J. (2003). Who goes to graduate school? Social and academic correlates of educational continuation after college. *Sociology of Education, 76*(2), 143–169.

Museus, S., Palmer, R., Davis, R., & Maramba, D. (2011). Racial and ethnic minority students' success in STEM education. *ASHE Higher Education Report, 36*(6). San Francisco, CA: Jossey-Bass.

National Center for Education Statistics. (2008). *Degree granting institutions, by control and type of institution.* U.S. Department of Education. Retrieved from http://nces.ed.gov/programs/digest/d08/tables/dt08_265.asp

Nerad, M., & Miller, D. (1996). Increasing student retention in graduate and professional programs. In J. Grant Haworth (Ed.), *Assessing graduate and professional education: Current realities, future prospects* (pp. 61–76). San Francisco, CA: Jossey-Bass.

Palmer, R., Maramba, D., & Gasman, M. (2012). *Fostering success of ethnic and racial minorities in STEM.* New York, NY: Routledge.

Reybold, L. E., & Alamia, J. (2008). Academic transitions in education: A developmental perspective of women faculty experiences. *Journal of Career Development, 35*(2), 107–128.

Rutledge, J., Carter-Veale, W., & Tull, R. (2011). Successful Ph.D. pathways to advanced STEM careers for Black women. In H. Frierson & W. Tate (Eds.), *Beyond stock stories and folktales: African-Americans' paths to STEM fields* (pp. 165–209). Bingley, United Kingdom: Emerald Group.

Sommers, D., & Franklin, J. C. (2012). Overview of projections to 2020. *Monthly Labor Review Online, 135*(1), 3–20. Retrieved from www.bls.gov/opub/mlr/2012/01/art1full.pdf

Sowell, R., Bell, N., & Zhang, T. (2008). *PhD completion project: Analysis of baseline demographic data.* Retrieved from www.cgsnet.org/ckfinder/userfiles/files/Data Sources_2008_07.pdf

Tierney, W. G. (1999). Models of minority college-going and retention: Cultural integrity versus cultural suicide. *Journal of Negro Education, 68*(1), 80–91.

Tsui, L. (2007). Effective strategies to increase diversity in STEM fields: A review of the research. *Journal of Negro Education, 76*(4), 555–581.

U.S. Census Bureau. (2011). *Population Division Table 2. Intercensal estimates of the resident population by sex, race, and Hispanic origin for the United States: April 1, 2000 to July 1, 2010* (US-EST00INT-02). Washington, DC: Author.

Vasquez, M., Lott, B., Garcia-Vazquez, E., Grant, S., Iwamasa, G., Molina, L. … Vestel-Dowdy, E. (2006). Personal reflections: Barriers and strategies for increasing diversity in psychology. *American Psychologist, 61*(2), 157–172.

EVA GRAHAM is the director for the California Institute of Technology's (Caltech) Center for Diversity.

NEW DIRECTIONS FOR HIGHER EDUCATION • DOI:10.1002/he

8

Foreign-born faculty play an important role in American doctoral education, contributing to the processes of internationalization and global collaboration.

Contributions of Foreign-Born Faculty to Doctoral Education and Research

Ketevan Mamiseishvili

Internationalization of higher education has been "an inevitable result of the globalized and knowledge-based economy of the 21st century" (Altbach & Teichler, 2001, p. 5). Globalization has pushed many U.S. higher education institutions to embrace internationalization as a central part of their mission, invest in resources and infrastructure to promote international education, and support exchanges of students and scholars across the world. The rise in the number of international faculty is one of the manifestations of these growing efforts of U.S. universities to compete for global talent and remain competitive in a globalized academic system.

As suggested by Manrique and Manrique (1999), foreign-born faculty members are "highly visible symbols of the changing face of the population in higher education" (p. 103). According to the data from the Institute of International Education (2011), there were 115,313 international scholars teaching or conducting research at U.S. colleges and universities in the 2010–2011 academic year. They were primarily concentrated in sciences and engineering disciplines, more specifically, biological and biomedical sciences (24.5%), health sciences (17.0%), engineering (12.9%), and physical sciences (11.5%). This is no surprise, considering that 67% of foreign nationals who received their doctorates in sciences and engineering from American institutions in 2005 were still in the United States in 2007 (Finn, 2010). Long-term stay rates of foreign-born doctorate holders in these fields reveal similar trends. For example, 62% of the 2002 cohort and 60% of the1997 cohort of foreign doctorate recipients still lived in the United States after five and ten years, respectively (Finn, 2010).

Kim, Twombly, and Wolf-Wendel (2012) even noted that the growth in the share of foreign-born faculty among new faculty hires exceeded the representation of domestic racial/ethnic minority groups. According to

NEW DIRECTIONS FOR HIGHER EDUCATION, no. 163, Fall 2013 © Wiley Periodicals, Inc.
Published online in Wiley Online Library (wileyonlinelibrary.com) • DOI:10.1002/he.20068

their calculations of the data from the Integrated Postsecondary Education Data System (IPEDS), in 2009, nonresident aliens made up 11.5% of the 11,599 new tenure-track faculty members at four-year institutions, followed by 10.5% Asian Americans, 0.5% African Americans, and 0.4% Hispanics (Kim et al., 2012). Additionally, foreign nationals make up the majority of postdoctoral fellows, which also signals the internationalization of the academic labor force in the United States (Cantwell, 2012).

Foreign-born faculty members are represented at all institutional types, but they tend to be more highly concentrated at research universities (e.g., Corley & Sabharwal, 2007; Kim, Wolf-Wendel, & Twombly, 2011; Mamiseishvili & Rosser, 2010; Marvasti, 2005). Evidence from the 2003 Survey of Doctorate Recipients (SDR) suggests that compared to U.S.-native faculty, international faculty were more likely to be employed at institutions that awarded more doctoral degrees (Kim et al., 2012). The data from the 2004 National Study of Postsecondary Faculty (NSOPF) also reveals that 58.8% of international faculty members were employed at research universities compared with only 35.6% of faculty who were U.S. citizens (Mamiseishvili & Rosser, 2010).

Research universities "assume unprecedented centrality in the knowledge-based world of the 21st century" (Altbach & Teichler, 2001, p. 5). Universities, through their doctoral education and research, "are increasingly seen as significant knowledge producers and thus as agents for economic growth" (Nerad, 2010, p. 3). Without a doubt, foreign-born faculty members who are employed at U.S. research universities make important contributions to the production of new knowledge and the training of the next generation of scholars. The goal of this chapter is to highlight these contributions through the lens of their research and engagement with students and examine the role foreign-born faculty members play in U.S. doctoral education.

Research and Scholarly Contributions

Significantly more attention has been devoted to examining foreign-born faculty members' contributions to science and research compared to other functions of their work, such as teaching, mentoring, or service. There seems to be a consensus among researchers that international faculty members are more productive in research compared to their U.S.-native peers (e.g., Corley & Sabharwal, 2007; Kim et al., 2011; Levin & Stephen, 1999; Mamiseishvili, 2010; Mamiseishvili & Rosser, 2010; Webber, 2012). One of the earliest studies that examined the impact of foreign-born and foreign-educated individuals on the U.S. scientific enterprise found that compared to U.S.-born peers, they were significantly more likely to make exceptional contributions to science and engineering (S&E), as measured by (1) the number of scientists elected to the National Academy of Sciences (NAS) and the National Academic of Engineering (NAE), (2) the most cited authors, (3) authors of frequently cited patents, and (4) founders of biotechnology firms (Levin & Stephen, 1999).

More recent studies of foreign-born academic scientists and engineers also confirmed that they were significantly more productive in research than their U.S.-born peers (Corley & Sabharwal, 2007). The data from the 2001 Survey of Doctorate Recipients (SDR) revealed higher levels of productivity for foreign-born academics on all research productivity measures in the dataset. Foreign-born scientists produced 2.09 refereed articles, .14 books, and 2.80 conference papers annually as compared to 1.64, .11, and 2.16, respectively, for U.S.-born scientists. Furthermore, foreign-born academics were more likely to receive more governmental research grants and patents relative to their U.S.-born peers (58% and 14.3% compared to 55.5% and 12%, respectively). Kim and colleagues' (2011) study of foreign-born faculty productivity, which examined the same 2001 SDR dataset, revealed similar results but only for those foreign-born faculty members who received their undergraduate degrees in their home countries. Interestingly, there was no significant difference in the productivity between U.S.-born faculty and those foreign-born faculty members who received their undergraduate degrees in the United States, indicating that these two groups were more likely to have had similar social, cultural, and academic experiences.

Comparable results emerged in the studies that examined the data from the NSOPF surveys (e.g., Lin, Pearce, & Wang, 2009; Mamiseishvili, 2010; Mamiseishvili & Rosser, 2010; Marvasti, 2005; Webber, 2012). The data from the 1993 and 1999 NSOPF in Marvasti's (2005) study revealed that foreign-born academics from all fields spent more time on research, displayed stronger preferences to allocate even more time to their scholarly pursuits, and consequently, produced more, especially in terms of refereed articles, than their native-born faculty colleagues. Based on the examination of a more recent NSOPF:04 dataset, Lin and colleagues (2009) also found that even after controlling for discipline, gender, and rank, foreign-born faculty were more productive in research than their U.S.-born colleagues (for example, 28 career refereed journal articles compared to 17). Similarly, studies by Mamiseishvili and Rosser (2010) and Webber (2012) concluded that foreign-born faculty at research universities directed more effort and time to research, and as a result, displayed higher research productivity. The same trend was observed when comparing female foreign-born faculty with their female U.S.-native peers (Mamiseishvili, 2010).

Thus, there is an abundance of evidence that foreign-born faculty members make significant contributions to the research function of U.S. doctoral-granting institutions. What is even more important to note is that not only that they themselves are more productive, but also, as Kim and colleagues (2011) found, that having international faculty as colleagues positively influenced U.S. faculty productivity as well. American faculty at a diverse campus (in terms of international faculty representation) were more productive than their colleagues at less internationalized peer institutions. Kim and her colleagues did not provide an explanation for this finding, but it is noteworthy that an internationalized campus was one of the institutional characteristics that led to increased faculty productivity in their study.

Furthermore, the national study of American faculty internationalization revealed that noncitizen faculty at U.S. institutions were significantly more likely to coauthor with their peers abroad (Finkelstein, Walker, & Chen, 2009). In general, Finkelstein and colleagues (2009) found that number of years spent abroad postbaccalaureate increased the likelihood of any faculty member engaging in research that was international in scope, collaborating and coauthoring with international scholars, and publishing in foreign countries. In other words, time spent abroad and exposure to international experiences in faculty members' adult life was the strongest socialization factor that led to faculty infusing international perspectives in their research.

No studies have examined the effect that research productivity of international faculty may have on the educational experiences of their doctoral students or postdoctoral fellows. One can assume that high research-grant productivity of foreign-born faculty will positively influence their students' ability to engage in research. Research grants acquired by faculty members often ensure that doctoral students have financial support to pursue their degrees and receive proper mentoring in the process of studying for their doctorates (Altbach, 2004). However, Libaers and Wang (2012) revealed that foreign-born faculty were very successful at securing funding and acquiring governmental grants for their own research, but they were less likely to commercialize their research and turn their inventions into marketable products. Based on the survey data from 1,795 academic scientists in the sciences and engineering, the study concluded that foreign-born faculty members were "entrepreneurial academics rather than academic entrepreneurs" (p. 267). The authors attributed the low levels of "commercial orientation" (p. 267) of foreign-born academics to their preference for more "curiosity-driven" rather than "use-inspired research" (p. 264) and their limited network of nonacademic peers. In sum, even though foreign-born faculty members' achievements and successes as researchers have been widely recognized and documented in the exiting research, there are still areas, such as their entrepreneurial performance, involvement with industry, or scholarly engagement with students, that need further exploration.

Teaching, Mentoring, and Program Development

As evidenced earlier, foreign-born academics through their research accomplishments make significant contributions to the strength of doctoral education in the United States. However, less is known about their involvement in teaching and mentoring of doctoral students. Previous studies have indicated that international faculty tend to be less involved in teaching, both at the undergraduate and graduate levels, compared to their U.S.-native peers (Mamiseishvili, 2010, 2011; Mamiseishvili & Rosser, 2010; Marvasti, 2005). But upon careful examination, Mamiseishvili (2011) found that significant differences in teaching involvement between the two groups were attributed to the total number of students taught, rather than to the assigned teaching responsibilities. For example, the data from NSOPF:04 revealed that at the graduate level, foreign-born faculty members taught a lower number of students per semester (19 versus 24), and consequently, generated significantly lower number of graduate student contact hours (75.30 versus 102.90) and student credit hours (60.08 versus 83.26) than their U.S.-born peers. Yet, there was no significant difference in terms of the amount of time they spent on teaching per week and the number of classroom credit hours assigned to them at the graduate level (Mamiseishvili, 2011).

Thus, significant differences in teaching workload between foreign-born and U.S.-born faculty members are less about how many classes they teach or how much time they spend on instruction. Difference seemed to be attributed more to the number of students enrolled in their courses. One of the plausible explanations for why foreign-born faculty members teach fewer numbers of students could be the types of classes they are assigned to teach (Mamiseishvili, 2011). For example, previous studies reported that foreign-born faculty in sciences and engineering often taught courses that were very technical in nature, and faculty in social sciences were frequently assigned courses that were related to their ethnic, cultural, or national background (Manrique & Manrique, 1999; Skachkova, 2007). It is hard to know for certain whether this is what accounts for the smaller enrollments in their classes, but it is possible that courses that are very technical in nature may not draw large numbers of students, or courses with international or foreign subject matter may be outside of the mainstream required coursework (Mamiseishvili, 2011).

It is through teaching and mentoring that foreign-born faculty can make the most significant contributions to the quality of doctoral students' educational experiences and to their socialization into the profession. Yet there has not been any research that focused specifically on the effectiveness of foreign-born faculty as teachers and mentors of doctoral students. However, despite this lack of evidence, several qualitative studies have explored what foreign-born faculty members' overall teaching experiences were like and how their students and colleagues perceived them as teachers; these studies may provide a glimpse into their teaching and advising roles in doctoral education (e.g., Gahungu, 2011; Skachkova, 2007; Thomas & Johnson, 2004). These studies suggest that differences in educational practices and cultural norms pose some challenges to foreign-born faculty in their classroom instruction and interactions with students (Thomas & Johnson, 2004). Teaching in a foreign culture may even be a more difficult task than conducting research. Luxon and Peelo (2009) discussed the "tension between the internationalism of research and the localism of teaching practices" (p. 651). While research is embedded in the "international disciplinary community of practice" (p. 658), teaching is entrenched in local educational practices, pedagogical settings, and expectations for teacher–student relationships that may not be familiar to international academics. Furthermore, accent may also adversely affect the teaching credibility of foreign-born faculty (Lippi-Green, 1999; Skachkova, 2007). Marvasti (2005) argued that perceptions about foreign-born faculty members' linguistic proficiency often influenced the judgments about their teaching effectiveness.

Despite these challenges, international faculty often bring pedagogical advantages to the teaching and learning process (Skachkova, 2007). For example, foreign-born faculty can draw on their cultural, linguistic, and national backgrounds and bring diverse perspectives to their classrooms. They often encourage their students to challenge taken-for-granted assumptions and look at issues from different angles. One of the foreign-born faculty members in Skachkova's (2007) phenomenological study explained that being from a different country "gave [her] an edge" in teaching and relations with students (p. 710). "Even by my appearance they realize that there is something else than America" (p. 710), she said. Foreign-born faculty frequently engage in a "border-crossing pedagogy," which Skachkova (2007) defines as pedagogy "that synthesizes traditional and new patterns of instruction and searches for innovative alternatives in the classroom" (p. 710).

International faculty members are also uniquely situated to expand their students' exposure to global perspectives and develop their international awareness and competence (Horn, Hendel, & Fry, 2007). Finkelstein and colleagues (2009) found that faculty who had lived abroad during their adulthood were more likely to integrate international content in their courses. The same could be said about international faculty members who tend to often travel abroad and maintain close ties with their friends and family in their home countries.

Foreign-born faculty can also serve as role models to the growing number of ethnic minority, immigrant, and international students pursuing doctoral degrees. Foreign-born academics in Skachkova's (2007) study had an ability to display a strong sense of empathy for their students. The struggles that they had themselves experienced as a foreigner trying to find a place in a new culture, adjust to a different educational environment, and overcome linguistic barriers gave them the ability to sympathize with their students and relate to their struggles and fears.

Finally, in regard to international faculty contributions to overall doctoral program improvement, there has not been a study that specifically examines to what extent international academics are engaged in curriculum review, programmatic improvements, or other leadership roles in their doctoral programs. However, several studies on international faculty productivity can provide some insight on their overall involvement in and satisfaction with their service roles. In general, prior research based on the NSOPF:04 data indicated that foreign-born faculty at research universities were less engaged in service, especially in administrative committee work (Mamiseishvili, 2010; Mamiseishvili & Rosser, 2010). Furthermore, they were significantly less satisfied with their authority to make curriculum decisions (Mamiseishvili, 2011). The earlier study using NSOPF:99 data by Wells, Seifert, Park, Reed, and Umbach (2007) also found that international faculty, especially those from the Middle East and Asia, were dissatisfied with their autonomy and authority to make decisions. The data from 2005–2008 COACHE (Collaborative on Academic Careers in Higher Education) faculty surveys from Harvard Graduate School of Education also revealed that pretenure noncitizen faculty were significantly less satisfied with their interactions with their colleagues (Kim et al., 2012).

Some qualitative research findings may provide explanations for foreign-born faculty members' limited involvement in and satisfaction with their service roles. For example, international faculty in Thomas and Johnson's (2004) study reported that they often felt "on the margins" and not part of an "in-group" (pp. 57–58). Some faculty felt that the respect and deference that they showed to their colleagues were interpreted as "lacking initiative and drive" (p. 60). Similarly, foreign-born women faculty in Skachkova's (2007) study often felt excluded from important decision-making processes and administrative service work; this exclusion limited their opportunities to have a say in the discussion of curricular or other key issues. Of course, these stories should not be generalized to all foreign-born faculty experiences in the United States, but this is definitely the area that warrants future research.

Implications for Policy, Practice, and Future Research

Higher education institutions, including their doctoral education programs, are increasingly functioning in a global context. In this context, doctoral education is not only responsible for preparing future generations of scholars and practitioners who are successful within the national boundaries but who can also effectively function across the borders (Nerad, 2010). Nerad (2011) argued that beyond traditional research skills and professional competencies, doctoral graduates need to possess cultural competencies to be able to communicate with scholars worldwide, participate in international scholarly communities, or work in multinational companies around the world. They need to have the necessary skills to be able to collaborate with international teams of scholars and deal with contemporary societal problems that can no longer be solved from just one country's perspective.

Foreign-born faculty members can serve as a critical resource for U.S. universities in their efforts to prepare the next generation of doctoral graduates. As Stohl (2007) noted, "In virtually every university system, the faculty in the academic departments hold the keys to education" (p. 367); therefore, the internationalization of higher education has to start with internationalizing the faculty. Finkelstein and colleagues (2009) found that on campuses where faculty members themselves led international initiatives, they were significantly more likely to engage in international research collaborations. Through their interactions with students, research collaborations, and engagement with community on and off campus, faculty members are best situated to advance international education initiatives and raise awareness of global issues (O'Hare, 2009). Faculty members who have themselves lived, learned, taught, or conducted research abroad are more likely to communicate the values of international education to their students, recognize and reward these experiences in their colleagues, and incorporate international perspectives in their own teaching and research (Finkelstein et al., 2009; O'Hare, 2009; Stohl, 2007).

Obviously, foreign-born faculty members are not and should not be the only ones responsible for leading the internationalization efforts at U.S. universities, but they are a valuable resource that doctoral programs should capitalize on. The majority of foreign-born faculty members come to the United States in their adult years after earning their undergraduate degrees in their home countries (Kim et al., 2012). They bring with them the knowledge of a different educational system, awareness of another culture, and an established network of peers and professional colleagues from their home countries. Through day-to-day interactions with foreign-born faculty, doctoral students have an opportunity to be exposed to these cultural, social, and pedagogical differences and to explore the possibilities for international connections and research collaborations without leaving their home campuses.

Of course, just hiring international faculty is not enough if they are not fully integrated in the teaching, research, and service functions of their academic departments and institutions. As indicated earlier, foreign-born faculty make significant contributions to research in terms of scholarly outputs they produce, including refereed publications and grants. However, less is known about their teaching and service engagement at the doctoral level. There is some indication that they teach less and are less involved in the administrative and decision-making functions than their colleagues, but there is little evidence as to why this may be the case or if this is even true for doctoral education. No prior research has focused specifically on the experiences of foreign-born faculty in doctoral education or has examined the perceptions of doctoral students about their interactions with foreign-born professors and mentors. Additionally, the scholarly community knows very little about the experiences and contributions of foreign-born faculty in disciplines outside of sciences and engineering. International academics in social sciences and education are less visible than their science and engineering faculty peers and may encounter some unique challenges or opportunities that need to be further explored (Gahungu, 2011).

NEW DIRECTIONS FOR HIGHER EDUCATION • DOI:10.1002/he

As Nerad (2011) states, "It takes a global village ... to develop tomorrow's PhDs and postdoctoral fellows" (p. 199). Foreign-born faculty members are important players in this "global village" at U.S. campuses. However, the responsibilities rest on both foreign-born faculty and their employing universities and departments. Foreign-born faculty themselves need to take initiative and seek leadership opportunities, instill the values of international education in their students, involve colleagues in their international peer networks, and "use their foreignness as an asset" (Gahungu, 2011, p. 1). On the other hand, administrators and other faculty need to create a more inclusive climate for foreign-born faculty and recognize and reward their contributions. Their "different way of knowing the world" (Skachkova, 2007, p. 710) can hold great potential for preparing the next generation of scholars in U.S. doctoral programs.

References

Altbach, P. G. (2004). Doctoral education: Present realities and future trends. *College and University, 80*(2), 3–10.

Altbach, P. G., & Teichler, U. (2001). Internationalization and exchanges in a globalized university. *Journal of Studies in International Education, 5*, 5–25.

Cantwell, B. (2012). Internationalization of academic labor: Considering postdocs. *International Higher Education, 69*, 17–19.

Corley, E. A., & Sabharwal, M. (2007). Foreign-born academic scientists and engineers: Producing more and getting less than their U.S.-born peers? *Research in Higher Education, 48*(8), 909–940.

Finkelstein, M. J., Walker, E., & Chen, R. (2009). The internationalization of the American faculty: Where are we, what drives or deters us? RIHE *International Seminar Reports, 13. The Changing Academic Profession over 1992–2007: International, Comparative, and Quantitative Perspectives.* Hiroshima, Japan: Research Institute for Higher Education, Hiroshima University.

Finn, M. G. (2010). *Stay rates of foreign doctorate recipients from U.S. universities, 2007.* Oak Ridge, TN: Oak Ridge Institute for Science and Education (ORISE). Retrieved from http://orise.orau.gov/files/sep/stay-rates-foreign-doctorate-recipients-2007.pdf

Gahungu, A. (2011). Integration of foreign-born faculty in academia: Foreignness as an asset. *International Journal of Educational Leadership Preparation, 6*(1), 1–21.

Horn, A. S., Hendel, D. D., & Fry, G. W. (2007). Ranking the international dimension of top research universities in the United States. *Journal of Studies in International Education, 11*(3/4), 330–358.

Institute of International Education. (2011). *Major field of specialization of international scholars, 2000/01–2010/11.* Open Doors Report on International Educational Exchange. Retrieved from www.iie.org/Research-and-Publications/Open-Doors/Data/International-Scholars/Major-Field-of-Specialization/1999-2010

Kim, D., Twombly, S., & Wolf-Wendel, L. (2012). International faculty in American universities: Experiences of academic life, productivity, and career mobility. In Y. J. Xu (Ed.), *New Directions for Institutional Research: No. 155. Refining the focus on faculty diversity in postsecondary institutions* (pp. 27–46). San Francisco, CA: Jossey-Bass.

Kim, D., Wolf-Wendel, L., & Twombly, S. (2011). International faculty: Experiences of academic life and productivity in U.S. universities. *Journal of Higher Education, 82*(6), 720–747.

Levin, S. G., & Stephen, P. E. (1999). Are the foreign born a source of strength for U.S. science? *Science, 285*(5431), 1–6.

Libaers, D., & Wang, T. (2012). Foreign-born academic scientists: Entrepreneurial academics or academic entrepreneurs? *R&D Management, 42*(3), 254–272.

Lin, Z., Pearce, R., & Wang, W. (2009). Imported talents: Demographic characteristics, achievement and job satisfaction of foreign-born full-time faculty in four-year American colleges. *Higher Education, 57*(6), 703–721.

Lippi-Green, R. (1999). *English with an accent: Language, ideology, and discrimination in the United States.* New York, NY: Routledge.

Luxon, T., & Peelo, M. (2009). Academic sojourners, teaching and internationalization: The experience of non-UK staff in a British University. *Teaching in Higher Education, 14*(6), 649–659.

Mamiseishvili, K. (2010). Foreign-born women faculty work roles and productivity at research universities in the United States. *Higher Education, 60*(2), 139–156. doi:10.1007/s10734-009-9291-0

Mamiseishvili, K. (2011). Teaching workload and satisfaction of foreign-born and U.S.-born faculty at four-year postsecondary institutions in the United States. *Journal of Diversity in Higher Education, 4*(3), 163–174. doi:10.1037/a0022354

Mamiseishvili, K., & Rosser, V. J. (2010). International and citizen faculty in the United States: An examination of their productivity at research universities. *Research in Higher Education, 51*(1), 88–107. doi:10.1007/s11162-009-9145-8

Manrique, C. G., & Manrique, G. G. (1999). *The multicultural or immigrant faculty in American society.* Lewiston, NY: The Edwin Mellen Press.

Marvasti, A. (2005). U.S. academic institutions and perceived effectiveness of foreign-born faculty. *Journal of Economic Issues, 39*(1), 151–176.

Nerad, M. (2010). Globalization and the internationalization of graduate education: A macro and micro view. *Canadian Journal of Higher Education, 40*(1), 1–12.

Nerad, M. (2011). It takes a global village to develop the next generation of PhDs and postdoctoral fellows. *Acta Academica Supplementum, 2,* 198–216. Retrieved from http://depts.washington.edu/cirgeweb/wordpress/wp-content/uploads/2012/11/NERAD-fin-Developing-the-Next-Generation-AASuppl2010_2_eversion-1.pdf

O'Hare, S. (2009). Vital and overlooked: The role of faculty in internationalizing U.S. campuses. In P. Blumenthal & R. Gutierrez (Eds.), *The Study Abroad White Paper Series, 6: Meeting America's Global Education Challenge* (pp. 38–45). New York, NY: Institute of International Education.

Skachkova, P. (2007). Academic careers of immigrant women professors in the U.S. *Higher Education, 53,* 697–738.

Stohl, M. (2007). We have met the enemy and he is us: The role of the faculty in the internationalization of higher education in the coming decade. *Journal of Studies in International Education, 11*(3/4), 359–372.

Thomas, J. M., & Johnson, B. J. (2004). Perspectives of international faculty members: Their experiences and stories. *Education and Society, 22*(3), 47–64.

Webber, K. L. (2012). Research productivity of foreign- and U.S.-born faculty: Differences by time on task. *Higher Education, 64*(5), 709–729.

Wells, R., Seifert, T., Park, S., Reed, E., & Umbach, P. D. (2007). Job satisfaction of international faculty in U.S. higher education. *Journal of the Professoriate, 2*(1), 5–32.

KETEVAN MAMISEISHVILI *is associate professor of higher education at the University of Arkansas.*

9

Diversity contributes to the development of an academic identity as well as the production of knowledge, both essential components of doctoral education.

How Diversity Influences Knowledge, Identity, and Doctoral Education

Karri A. Holley

The goal of this volume was to expand readers' understanding of diversity in doctoral education. Chapter authors considered not only the role of racial, ethnic, and gender diversity, but also the diversity of institutional type, academic discipline, social ecology, and professional context. Our intent was to acknowledge the numerous factors that influence access and participation among different student groups while also bringing other categories of difference to the forefront. While enrollment data that reflect such categories as gender and ethnicity are easily measurable indications of diversity, other areas exist that demand attention. By adding nuanced complexity to the issue of diversity, the authors sought to provide guideposts for future research, policy, and practice in this area.

Two underlying assumptions throughout this volume are that diversity has value and that such value is an essential component of higher education institutions. As one example, students become aware of different global perspectives when they interact with diverse peers. Gurin, Dey, Hurtado, and Gurin (2002) wrote, "Colleges that diversify their student bodies and institute policies that foster genuine interaction across race and ethnicity provide the first opportunity for many students to learn from peers with different cultures, values, and experiences" (p. 336). This engagement is furthered when students are challenged by a curriculum that fosters critical thinking and cultural awareness. Not only do students as individuals benefit from this development, but so also does the institution, as well as larger society. "A key impetus for linking diversity with central educational and civic goals is to better position the next generation of leaders for the project of advancing social progress," suggested Hurtado (2007, p. 186).

Doctoral programs play a critical role in higher education's mission to advance educational and civic goals. These programs make possible an

NEW DIRECTIONS FOR HIGHER EDUCATION, no. 163, Fall 2013 © Wiley Periodicals, Inc.
Published online in Wiley Online Library (wileyonlinelibrary.com) • DOI:10.1002/he.20069

institution's capacity to produce innovative research and new knowledge. By providing training that enables doctoral students to engage in complex environments, universities are playing an active role in the emerging global knowledge-based economy. "New PhDs are expected not only to know how to do research, but to also be competent writers, speakers, managers, and team members who can communicate research goals and results effectively inside and outside the university," concluded Nerad (2010, p. 79). The changing role of higher education as part of this economy is accompanied by changes in how doctoral students are socialized to be a member of the discipline and the academic profession. Producing scientists across the disciplines who can visualize new and innovative ways of approaching their work is a dominant paradigm for 21st-century doctoral education.

Diversity, then, should feature prominently in conversations about the changing nature of doctoral education. Who is involved in the process is just as important as the process itself. By admitting students who complete their undergraduate studies at a range of institutional types, for example, or supporting research that extends topics even further than popular disciplinary norms, institutions actively define their teaching, learning, and public service missions. In this conclusion, I offer reflections on diversity and doctoral education. I summarize common themes from the preceding chapters by considering (1) diversity of knowledge and (2) diversity of identity. This approach is neither to diminish the influence of individual demographics nor to suggest that people with a shared demographic have a similar approach to knowledge production. Rather, people bring an individual diversity to social institutions, shaped by their unique life experiences. The social, cultural, and economic effects on knowledge require higher education to be deliberate in its efforts to recruit a diverse faculty and student body (Hurtado, 2007). A publication by the National Academy of Engineering (NAE; 2002) offered this argument: "Creativity is simply making unexpected connections between things we already know, bound by life experiences ... [diverse life experiences] are the 'gene pool' out of which creativity comes" (p. 12).

Diversity of Knowledge

If knowledge is the operating core of the higher education organization, then the ability to diversify knowledge is an essential aspect of organizational growth and development. This perspective challenges the nature of the academic disciplines as traditional communities of practice that privilege ways of knowing about the world. Academic practices are shaped by these disciplinary traditions in ways that become normative (Becher & Trowler, 2001). Part of the strength of the disciplines and their significant role in the development of higher education has been their ability to maintain boundaries and focus on questions of depth and significance. However, as Becher and Trowler (2001) acknowledged, "Structures have the characteristics of both rules and resources" (p. 1). Those same structures that have provided the resources for the academic disciplines to flourish have also restricted the means and content of knowledge production.

A foundational question for observers interested in doctoral education is the relationship between diversity and knowledge. Does fostering diversity in doctoral education produce distinct outcomes in terms of knowledge that are more beneficial than those outcomes produced in environments that lack diversity? Evidence from studies of organizational behavior indicate that difference is a valuable feature in the ways that individuals interact with each other and one that promotes enhanced work group outcomes. Milliken and Martins (1996) offered empirical data to suggest that racial diversity among group members facilitated higher group-level cognitive outcomes than homogenous groups, a gain that also existed for diverse nationalities. Even academic disciplines that do not require doctoral students to work as part of a research team can benefit from the interaction of diverse others. Students experience the discipline through classrooms, professional conferences, and other forms of social networks. "Social interaction among diverse perspectives can lead to the emergence of new insights through conceptual restructuring within the groups," concluded Jehn, Northcraft, and Neale (1999, p. 743).

Milliken and Martins (1996) also noted that the organizational context in which diverse teams interact has important influences on team outcomes. They concluded, "The context in which the group is interacting is a critical, and understudied, variable likely to affect how the diversity or heterogeneity of a group affects outcomes" (p. 419). This conclusion reminds us that students benefit not only from interactions with diverse individuals but also from working within an institution that values diversity and commits resources to facilitating engagement between diverse others. Given the norms of socialization so prevalent within doctoral education, students are more likely to value diversity of knowledge when such diversity is valued by the department, the discipline, and the institution.

Knowledge is not neutral, and recognizing that knowledge exhibits characteristics reflective of the sociocultural context brings an important perspective to our understanding of diversity. One example suggests that gender remains a formidable obstacle for female scholars. Even when they hold the same qualifications, women in masculine occupations such as engineering are perceived to be less competent than their male peers (American Association of University Women, 2010). This perception is associated with being disliked by colleagues as well as a greater likelihood that the woman will leave the occupation. Katila and Merilainen (1999) observed, "The history of science can be seen as literature written by men, for men, and about men" (p.165). Disciplines outside the sciences that are considered more feminine in nature, such as education, social work, and nursing, still exist within the institutional confines of the academy and therefore are subject to similar forces about the definition of valuable knowledge.

New Directions for Higher Education • DOI:10.1002/he

Additional evidence suggests that racial and ethnic identities impact external recognition of a researcher's scholarship. Carlone and Johnson (2007) wrote, "It is much easier to get recognized as a scientist if your ways of talking, looking, acting, and interacting align with the historical and prototypical notions of a scientist" (p. 1207). By extension, recognition of competence is also associated with these prototypical notions of science. Given the bidirectional flow of identity development, in that identity is shaped not only by how one sees his or her self, but also how others see that person, then rewards for knowledge competency are a crucial part of doctoral education.

Diversity of Identity

I now turn to the question of identity and its role in doctoral education. Scholar and urban activist Jane Jacobs (1961, p. 164) hinted at the benefits of diversity when she wrote that the "everyday, ordinary performance of mixing people" creates complex "pools of use" that are greater than the sum of their parts. Increased diversity has the potential to facilitate innovation by bringing together a broad range of perspectives, insights, and ideas that can be applied across the academic disciplines. Raskin (in Jacobs, 1961) concluded, "It is the richness of human variation that gives vitality and color to the human setting" (p. 229). Drawing from research in areas of urban planning and development, scholars such as Florida (2003) have championed the relationship between creative capital and regional development. Put simply, by bringing together a diverse community of educated and productive people, communities experience growth in economic criteria such as income level, industry growth, and overall employment. Florida identifies three crucial elements to the geography of creativity: technology, talent, and tolerance. By welcoming a diverse population and offering the tools to support innovative ideas, creative communities flourish.

The application of creative capital to higher education suggests similar advantages for knowledge production. First, by supporting doctoral students financially, as well as supporting access to the technology needed to facilitate their learning, research institutions indicate their commitment to the future generation of scholars. This argument moves beyond the notion of technology as a specific piece of equipment or software. Rather, it calls attention to multiple ways in which a task can be accomplished. Doctoral students are recognized as valuable members of the academic community when institutions facilitate their work through campus space, adequate compensation, and cultural rewards. Second, the concept of talent suggests that universities recruit doctoral students who bring with them a range of academic and professional expertise. While previous academic success is an important indicator of talent, other indicators could include community engagement or professional achievements. Moving beyond those traditional indicators requested during the graduate admissions process can be challenging for universities and academic departments and requires conversation about the unique cultural dimensions of the department as well as the institution. Finally, tolerance is an essential social element to facilitating creativity. As defined by Florida (2003), tolerance reflects "openness, inclusiveness, and diversity to all ethnicities, races, and walks of life" (p. 10). By adopting Florida's framework, my intent is not to suggest that the outcomes of doctoral education are purely quantitative, such as the financial gains seen through fostering economic innovation. Rather, I suggest that those qualitative indicators of difference provide a productive and fertile environment for knowledge.

Traditionally, higher education has privileged a specific notion of identity in relation to knowledge production. What are the cultural models of success within the discipline, and how are those models developed? Often male, and predominantly White, this scholarly identity was assumed to reside safe within the ivory walls of the institution, free from the possible biasing effects of outside influences. This identity enabled students and scholars to engage with knowledge in a manner that was objective and logical. Knowledge flowed in only one direction, from the university to the communities outside its ivory towers. The academic disciplines have been shaped by this pervasive scholarly identity. For example, in the science and engineering disciplines, students are taught in ways that are perceived to be neutral in terms of personal characteristics such as race, class, and gender (Johnson, 2007). This neutrality not only perpetuates the idea of knowledge as objective and free from bias, but also suggests an ideal academic identity.

Other challenges to identity development and diversity within the academy were outlined by Pinel, Warner, and Chua (2005), who documented such issues as stigma-consciousness that influence inclusion on campus. When diversity is lacking, those few students who exhibit diverse characteristics bear unrealistic burdens. For example, Pinel, Warner, and Chua noted that minority men enrolled in a predominantly White institution experience race-based stigma-consciousness that can result in poor academic performance and a tendency to disengage from campus life. The resulting challenges related to inclusion and academic success have been well documented (Garces, 2012; Smith, 2009). Students are socialized early during their educational experiences as to the academic ideal. When they do not see themselves reflected in this ideal and are subsequently discouraged (either implicitly or explicitly) from further study in the field, distinctions are made in terms of who is qualified to serve as a full-fledged member of the academic community (Archer et al., 2010).

Implications and Conclusion

A starting point for diversity in doctoral education is the admission of a diverse student population. Given the nature of graduate studies, however, attention must be given to all facets of the academic pipeline. As several authors in this volume have indicated, the pathway to doctoral education is shaped by educational experiences throughout the student's life. In addition to student diversity, the curriculum plays a significant role in shaping the way scholars view their discipline and the world around them. Doctoral students should not only be introduced to a range of knowledge but also to a range of pedagogies for extending that knowledge to future classrooms. Given the importance of diversity as part of the institutional context, academic departments and universities are also tasked to demonstrate the cultural value of the concept. Doctoral students experience a developmental process that shapes the way they view themselves as scholars and members of the academic discipline, as well as their views on higher education more broadly.

For those researchers interested in the theory and practice of doctoral education, a greater attention to the multiple facets of diversity provides valuable insight. In this chapter, I have demonstrated that diversity exists beyond single indicators of difference and shapes the way we define knowledge and identify other members of the academy. "Diversity is a powerful agent of change," observed Smith (2009, p. 3), "one that can serve as a facilitator of institutional mission and social purpose." Given the essential role that doctoral education serves in the growth and development of the American higher education system, attention to diversity within this segment is crucial.

References

American Association of University Women. (2010). *Why so few? Women in science, technology, engineering, and mathematics.* Washington, DC: Author.

Archer, L., Dewitt, J., Osborne, J., Dillon, J., Willis, B., & Wong, B. (2010). "Doing" science versus "being" a scientist: Examining 10/11 year old schoolchildren's constructions of science through the lens of identity. *Science Education, 94*(4), 617–639.

Becher, T., & Trowler, P. (2001). *Academic tribes and territories* (2nd ed.). Philadelphia, PA: Open University Press.

Carlone, H., & Johnson, A. (2007). Understanding the science experiences of successful women of color: Science identity as an analytic lens. *Journal of Research in Science Teaching, 44*(8), 1187–1218.

Florida, R. (2003). Cities and the creative class. *City & Community, 2*(1), 3–19.

Garces, L. (2012). Racial diversity, legitimacy, and the citizenry: The impact of affirmative action bans on graduate school enrollment. *Review of Higher Education, 36*(1), 93–132.

Gurin, P., Dey, E., Hurtado, S., & Gurin, G. (2002). Diversity and higher education: Theory and impact on educational outcomes. *Harvard Educational Review, 72*(3), 330–367.

Hurtado, S. (2007). Linking diversity with the educational and civic missions of higher education. *Review of Higher Education, 30*(2), 185–196.

Jacobs, J. (1961). *The death and life of great American cities.* New York, NY: Random House.

Jehn, K., Northcraft, G., & Neale, M. (1999). Why differences make a difference: A field study of diversity, conflict, and performance in workgroups. *Administrative Science Quarterly, 44*(4), 741–763.

Johnson, A. (2007). Unintended consequences: How science professors discourage women of color. *Science Education, 91*(5), 805–821.

Katila, S., & Merilainen, S. (1999). A serious researcher or just another nice girl? Doing gender in a male-dominated scientific community. *Gender, Work, and Organization, 6*(3), 163–173.

Milliken, F., & Martins, L. (1996). Searching for common threads: Understanding the multiple effects of diversity in organizational groups. *Academy of Management Review, 21*(2), 402–433.

National Academy of Engineering. (2002). *Diversity in engineering: Managing the workforce of the future.* Washington, DC: National Academies Press.

Nerad, M. (2010, October). *The internationalization of doctoral education—A two-way approach: Promoting productive educational experiences for PhD students.* Paper presented at the AC21 International Forum 2010. Retrieved from www.ac21.org /files/7213/2730/0845/IF2010-Report.pdf#page=84

Pinel, E., Warner, L., & Chua, P. (2005). Getting there is only half the battle: Stigma consciousness and maintaining diversity in higher education. *Journal of Social Issues, 61*(3), 481–506.

Smith, D. (2009). *Diversity's promise for higher education: Making it work.* Baltimore, MD: Johns Hopkins University Press.

KARRI A. HOLLEY *is associate professor and coordinator of the Higher Education Program at the University of Alabama, where she also serves on the advisory board for the Tide Together Graduate Student Mentoring Program.*

New Directions for Higher Education • DOI:10.1002/he

INDEX

Page references followed by *fig* indicate an illustrated figure; followed by *t* indicate a table.